# DEFYING GRAVITY

JOE SIKORRA

# DEFYING GRAVITY

How Choosing Joy Lifted
My Family from
Death to Life

IGNATIUS PRESS    SAN FRANCISCO

Cover photo courtesy of author

Cover design by Enrique J. Aguilar Pinto

© 2018 by Ignatius Press, San Francisco
All rights reserved
ISBN 978-1-62164-145-2
Library of Congress Control Number 2017941950
Printed in the United States of America ∞

*To Dr. Gerald Berkman, the boys' pediatrician, who made himself available to us day and night from the beginning; Bobby Moin, who provided care to our boys with such a generous heart we could never repay him; and our village, which has made this journey with us*

# CONTENTS

# INTRODUCTION

It is said that what doesn't kill you makes you stronger. I believe it is also true that what can and *will* kill you can make you stronger. My beautiful sons are living proof of this statement.

In 1998, when our older son, John, turned seven, my wife, Lori, and I shared a parent's worst nightmare: "Your son has a neurological disease. It is fatal," the specialist said.

I don't remember everything he said. For that matter, I don't remember the doctor or anything else of substance about the meeting. "Fatal" is all I remember. It was as if all the oxygen and the warmth had been sucked out of the room. Lori and I couldn't think. We couldn't breathe. Shocked, we collapsed into the sterile chairs in the doctor's office. They offered no relief from the weight that had been dropped on us. Emotion crept up from our innermost being, and we gave way to a torrent of tears. We tried to gulp in air through our sobs as the doctors explained the horrible progression of the disease: blindness, seizures, feeding tubes, loss of motor and cognitive function, and John's death in his late teens or early twenties. The common name for this most uncommon of diseases is juvenile Batten disease.

Our hearts had been dealt an unimaginable blow from which I could not imagine recovery. It couldn't be worse. Right?

Wrong. Six months later we were told that our other son, Ben, four years old, suffered from the same debilitating disease. Both of our children would spend their entire short lives increasingly burdened by the disease's ravaging effects. We had no idea how we could find a path through this dark valley, knowing it could lead only to death. If hope is believing in the good one can't yet see, what hope could we find, given the bleak picture the doctors painted for us? The doctors said much but gave nothing. How could we watch our children, flesh of our flesh and bone of our bone, dwindle and die and not die ourselves?

"How tragic. How awful," one might say. Yes, it certainly seemed that way to us. But we discovered that overflowing love can coexist with heartbreak and abundant joy can live side by side with suffering. These apparent contradictions can be experienced at the same time within the same family.

"Impossible," one might think. But it is possible for a heart transformed and molded by God.

Lori and I were raised in faith–filled homes. We believed in a kind, loving God. We paid homage to Him every Sunday. But the faith necessary to see and to experience the beauty in the road that lay ahead of us would need to be forged in the fire of adversity. And this adversity, in the form of our children's disease, was the gift we were given.

"Gift?"

Yes, a most precious gift. I wouldn't trade my life experience, my family, for the world.

Of course, from day one we begged God to heal our boys. If I could have given my life for theirs, I would have. But God didn't allow me to trade places with them. He gave me not the opportunity to die for them but the chance to *live* for them. How could I live for them? By accepting Christ's death on the Cross for me and my family and by letting go of my old self and putting on fullness of life in Christ.

Although my family's chief struggle has been living with a terminal disease, this story is not about death and dying. Rather, it is a story of life and living. It is an adventure story, in which hardship meets joy, love embraces tears, and laughter rises amid despair.

Families and marriages, understandably, often crumble under the weight of crushing circumstances. To avoid that fate, my family needed to learn how to face the battles of each day by *choosing* courage in face of fear, faith in the thick of doubt, hope in the pit of despair, and love when we felt ready to give up. We didn't always win. Sometimes fear, dejection, and depression ruled the day. Knowing that the battle would be long and victory would never be assured, discouragement sometimes got the better of us. Yet our lives continued to be increasingly enriched. Does that seem impossible? Well, as the Good Book says, "With God all things are possible" (Mt 19:26).

Saint Paul the Apostle, in his Letter to the Philippians (chapter 4), says that he had learned to be content no matter his circumstances; that he had found the recipe for being happy. Happiness is not found by avoiding struggles, he discovered, but by embracing them and letting God do amazing things with us. That has been our experience; that has been our story.

# The First Real Miracle

In 1991, when our first son was born, Lori and I had been married for four years and were living in Santa Monica, California. Our lives were idyllic. I was living out my dream of becoming an actor, and Lori had a good job as a nurse. Our small studio, built in the 1920s and sporting old pine floors, was blocks from the beach and from our church, Saint Monica's, where we had begun to build a community based on supportive friendships.

With our Saint Monica's group, we had barbecues and huge Thanksgiving feasts with about twelve of us crammed into our little apartment. We became close with a couple of our priests. There was always something going on in our parish, and every once in a while, the celebration went a little too far. For example, the pastor banned us from having parties on the upper floor of the rectory after he found marks where Lori had roller-skated on the wood floors (we are still trying to pretend that never happened).

For the most part, Lori and I did a pretty good job of living simply and in the moment. We understood that our joy would not be greater if we had more stuff but would be made complete whenever we focused on being grateful for what we had.

We had grown up in Florida. I had always loved being a clown (not the kind with a painted face) and getting attention. I was creative and couldn't see myself behind a desk. So after a year of junior college, during which I managed to pass a couple of physical education classes, I packed my sandals and a pair of jeans, filled my very cool black Camaro (a manual four-speed with about 12,000 horsepower) with gas (affordable at that time), and moved to New York. (Actually, it was New Jersey, but New York sounds so much more impressive.) My name in lights—that's what I thought would satisfy my inflated ego. Or maybe that was a way to serve my fragile ego: "Look at me, everyone! Tell me I'm wonderful (because I don't quite believe it myself)."

I met with some early success: modeled in Calvin Klein ads, shot a bunch of commercials, and deepened my knowledge and love of acting. I began to see it as a calling. Or maybe I just fell more in love with the idea of being rich and famous. Anyway, I couldn't imagine doing anything else with my life professionally.

While in New York, I flirted with the production side of things. My buddies and I made some short comedic videos using Matchbox cars mixed with real cars and bad sound effects. We laughed so hard that we usually ran out of light before we ran out of ridiculous ideas to shoot. But acting remained my first love.

New York was great for modeling and theater, but I wanted to pursue film and television. My face on the screen seemed more appealing than my name in lights. And besides, this Florida boy was really missing the sun and the ocean. With about $250 in my pocket, my piano keyboard in the backseat, and a full tank of gas, in 1986, I drove three thousand miles to the West Coast. Lori followed me to California the next year, after completing college at Florida State.

Lori had made the wise decision to get her degree in nursing so that she would have a real job upon graduation, and she found one—at a hospital—when she landed in California. A few months later, we said the really big "I do." It was a great start: her practicality and good sense were a terrific balance to my dreaminess—and so, as I was about to learn, was her choice of a career that involved caring for the sick and the dying.

Her dad had encouraged her in her career because he wanted her to have the stability he never knew. "I always lived with the fear of losing our house growing up, of just barely having enough," Lori had said. "I want the security of a real job." I think what she slowly discovered was that money alone would never provide security enough to overcome fear. But it did help to keep the house.

We spent our early married years living simply but well. It's wonderful when you can embrace poverty in exchange for the wealth of life experiences. Home was found in each other's arms and with the newfound family we had discovered in the people around us—in our church and our neighbors.

I was thrilled to be paid for doing make-believe, but acting jobs are few and far between, and this reality had real consequences. The first was financial—I wasn't earning a paycheck every two weeks. The other was psychological—the few days I worked each year were not enough to make me feel as though I were really *doing* something. As a result, a not-so-strange thought occurred to me: I didn't want to pretend for a living; I wanted to do something real, something that would help me to hold down my end of the family financial bargain. Without completely abandoning the hope of steady employment—an oxymoron for most actors—I decided to go back to school to make myself more financially marketable. With about two college credits already under my belt, I—ever the optimist—felt I was well on my way to great scholarly heights when I enrolled in classes at the local community college.

One of my first courses was in criminal justice, taught by a captain in the Santa Monica Police Department. From him I learned that I could become a reserve police officer and enjoy all the risk of being a cop without the pay. Perfect! (I did mention that practicality was Lori's thing, not mine.)

Off to the academy I went. Five months later, I hit the streets, working with some of the best friends I would ever have. This work was more than just pretend. The bad guys carried real guns, and so did I. No director yelled, "Cut!" at the end of a particularly harrowing scene, but if luck would have it, I went home safely.

I worked on patrol, in undercover narcotics, and with the K-9 unit (undoubtedly my favorite). I got to ride ATVs on the beach and do other cool stuff. The job gave me the chance to serve and to stand up to bullies, while allowing me to pursue my dream of acting. Working as a reserve cop opened my eyes to the struggles of others, and I saw the devastating effects of addiction and violence.

I appreciated the camaraderie that evolves from a shared mission, from standing, working, and striving with others who are fighting the good fight. I experienced success not as an individual but in partnership with others, as a member of a team. I wasn't on the streets to be a star. Fame could never be the goal of good police work. The mission is what matters.

Answer the call. Respond to the need. Stop the threat. Defend the innocent. Help the helpless. These are the duties of the police officer, and they taught me how to live for others. Paradoxically, as I learned to live less for my own ego and more for others, I began to flourish as a person. I can't say that I mastered selflessness, but I made progress in that department, and it felt good.

So many of the messages around us—in advertising, on social media, and from self-help gurus—suggest that happiness is found in doing what is best for oneself. But Jesus gave His disciples contrary advice:

> If any man would come after me, let him deny himself and take up his cross and follow me. For whoever would save his life will lose it, and whoever loses his life for my sake will find it. For what will it profit a man, if he gains the whole world and forfeits his life? Or what shall a man give in return for his life? (Mt 16:24–26)

Doing police work, I was just beginning to understand what Jesus meant.

At the end of each shift, as I hung my uniform in the locker, I thanked God for the experiences of that day. Yet, as much as I found the adventure and the service rewarding, I doubted I was put on earth to be a cop. In police work I was constantly confronted with the darkness in this world, and that conflict was wearing me down. It took more than it gave back. It seemed to me that the work I was meant to do would invigorate and satisfy me even when it was difficult, the way my occasional acting jobs did. Thus, I found myself longing again to fulfill my ambition to be an actor.

During this time, Lori and I were settled into our community and made enough money to put food on the table and to pay the bills. Although we didn't have much in the way of material wealth, in moments of grace we realized that we had all we needed. Our home was about two hundred square feet—we didn't have a baby room; we had one room—and it seemed to be enough. The only thing we lacked was a child. We realized that our lives were a little self-indulgent. We were responsible to no one but each other. We pretty much did what we wanted, when we wanted.

The "baby" conversation between us probably went something like this:

Lori: "I think it's time ..."

Me: "Okay!"

But, Lori explained, I needed to understand that making a baby meant making the commitment to nurture another person besides ourselves, to make the move from selfish love to *selfless* love. I didn't fully understand it all. Who does? But I was eager.

Therefore, we agreed that it was time to expand our little family, even though we didn't know how having a child would work. I mean, we knew how our reproductive systems worked, but we didn't know how our being parents together would work.

To support my dream of being an actor, Lori was working to help pay the bills, and I was grateful for her sacrifice. Yet when she asked if I would stay home with a baby while she worked, I was wary of becoming a Mr. Mom. When she asked if we could return to Florida so that we might have a simpler life and more support from our extended families, I resisted. Returning to Florida would cost me my dream of acting and what I understood as my calling in life. To me the price seemed too high; to Lori the price seemed a practical necessity.

This difference between us caused a fair amount of tension and resentment. Distance began to set in. Yet with the future unpredictable and the present uncomfortable, we just kept doing what was in front of us and marched on: we stayed in California, and we tried to have a baby.

Lori became pregnant easily. We were overjoyed. We were excited about the future. With each pound she gained, I thought she looked more beautiful. I told her so, but probably not often enough.

"Honey, I think you look really sexy."

"Get away from me. I feel like a cow."

"Babe, honestly, you don't look like a cow."

With years and wisdom, my comebacks got better; otherwise we would be divorced by now.

She had morning sickness morning, noon, and night. I put my hand on her forehead while she was throwing up as though that would help. She was a trooper. I'm convinced that if men had to go through pregnancy and childbirth, we would have no population growth. Or more accurately, no population at all.

We took the obligatory Lamaze classes. Men, don't be confused here. This was not *Le Mans*, the car race. No, this was a lesson on breathing during contractions and administering ice chips.

The pregnancy went smoothly with no complications—that is, if something the size of a bowling ball growing inside a woman's body can be considered uncomplicated.

After about a day of labor, Lori's doctor said that our son John wasn't going to come out naturally. "We'll have to perform a C-section," he said. "His shoulders are too big."

"That's my boy," I replied proudly. Lori looked at me with daggers in her eyes.

The birth of my son was the greatest miracle I had ever witnessed. When I held him in my arms, I felt giddy with excitement. He looked perfect. His flesh against mine felt so smooth and soft, so delicate and tender. How could this fragile covering protect him from life's harshness? His baby's breath smelled of life. Friends brought champagne to celebrate, but I was already intoxicated—with the pure, rich emotion of being grateful for life.

Some say we should live each day as though it were our last. But what if we celebrated each day as though it were our first? What if we looked at the world with wonder and embraced it with simple trust? What if we relished being comforted with a gentle touch? What if we fell asleep and awoke without worry and stress?

I didn't know how to act in the hospital. I was a good actor, but I was an amateur on this stage. I felt as though I had to ask permission to see my child, to hold him, while everyone else seemed to know what to do: how to wrap him in a blanket, how to change his diaper, how to comfort him. I didn't even know what I didn't know. Even so, I fell in love with my son and trusted that love would teach me what I needed to know.

When the baby came home, it was officially time for the kids (Lori and me) to grow up. Well, not really, but it was definitely time for more living space. We moved about five feet away into a one-bedroom apartment in the same complex.

John cried a lot as a newborn. The neighbors complained, and it became clear that even in the new apartment we were quickly running out of room. By the grace of God, and a very kind building owner, we moved into a big apartment about six blocks away.

After a few months, the screaming subsided, and Lori and I discovered we were stewards of a child who seemed almost angelic, otherworldly. Baby John would use his tiny hand to caress his ear gently. Then, looking deeply into our eyes, as though he wanted to share some precious gift he possessed, he would reach up and gently caress ours. He knew how to soothe himself, and very early on we witnessed how his touch, his presence, soothed others as well. We didn't know it at the time, but that quality would never change with him. The beauty of this simple soul would transform lives. He didn't need to cultivate this goodness; it was a gift he was given—a gift he would share. And it blossomed. I began to see that a gift held selfishly dies, but gifts that are shared grow.

John met one of his dearest friends, Cameron, days after birth. Lori and Kay, Cameron's mom, met at a Mommy and Me class. Our families bonded instantly. We cared for and loved each other's children as they grew. We supported and encouraged one another when parenting seemed overwhelming. Brent, Cameron's dad, taught the boys to surf just after they had learned to swim. Lori and I were the godparents of Catherine, Brent and Kay's eldest daughter. We were present at many firsts—first steps, first days of school, first scraped knees.

During John's early years we spent many warm days on the beach with Brent and Kay and other parents of young children. Maybe the stink of too many soiled diapers drove us outside, but the beach was our favorite place for rejuvenation and fun. We and our friends would pack up beach umbrellas and playpens for the babies to nap in, and we would collaborate on the food: someone would bring bread, another would bring pasta, and yet another would pack cold beers or a bottle of wine. The parents got the chance to swim or surf while the babies learned to eat sand. We watched sunsets over the Pacific. We basked in the glow of blossoming friendships.

This time was beautiful in its simplicity. Later, Lori would refer to it as the "sweet spot days". She had been counseled by a wise older woman to say no to all the volunteer jobs and yes to her kids. "Enjoy these times and don't wish them away," the woman had said, "for they will disappear all on their own one day soon." These words proved to be both sensible and prophetic.

But Lori and I also faced challenges during these wonder days. We had some difficulty adjusting to our new roles as parents. (To be precise, I had trouble, which caused Lori trouble.) My acting work was sporadic, but I was passionate about it and still dreamed of turning it into a full-time profession. I feared that if I gave any more of myself to something other than my work, I would decrease my chances of success. And the odds of my success were already heavily stacked against me, as they would have been for anyone trying to make it as an actor in Southern California.

I was probably more involved in John's day-to-day life than were many fathers, at that time, in their children's lives, and I feared that giving even more of myself to child-care would make me, well, less of a man. So I held back. I didn't support Lori as I should have; doing what needs to be done for the sake of one's family is what grown-ups do. I had much growing up to do.

The involved father role wasn't something I would be able to learn from my dad's example. His work was outside the home. My mom, God bless her, did the vast majority of taking care of the house and the kids. So I had to blaze my own trail, and that took a lot of trial and error.

When I look back now, I can see that my fears were unwarranted and a waste of time. In fact, the closeness that grew out of those early bonding years, the diaper-changing years, the holding and comforting years, would serve me beautifully. I learned to love more deeply and to give of myself more completely. In short, those years helped me to get out of myself and into the other—an essential ingredient of any successful relationship. But I was a slow learner.

# 2

# Life and Death

When John was a year old, Lori's father was diagnosed with lung cancer. He had started smoking when he was about fifteen and never turned back. Like most smokers, he realized that the habit was not good for his health, but he had become too addicted to quit.

Lori's father was a simple, hardworking man. His pleasures outside his family were few. When he wasn't desperately trying to eke out a living in his shop, he occasionally went fishing or crabbing (Lori's favorite activity with him). I don't think catching the creatures was that important to him. He stood along the water's edge, or on the pier, and looked out. Maybe he was looking ahead at what he hoped would be; maybe he was searching the past for what he hoped had been. I don't know. But this dreamy quality of his Lori saw in me.

All inventions and works of art begin with a dream or a vision: seeing what can be but does not yet exist. Dreams aren't reality. They are thoughts of the possible coupled with belief. Although great achievements begin with dreams, living too much in dreams can keep us from the important work of the here and now.

The theme of this chapter is life and death. John was born—life. Lori's dad was terminally ill—death. Along with these was the story of life and death ongoing within ourselves. Lori and I continued to struggle with how to divide the childcare duties. We longed for greater financial security and a house to call our own. Meanwhile, my career did not progress as we had hoped. We had begun the agonizing process of dying and being reborn, and, looking back, we marveled at how our life together had started out so easy.

Lori and I began dating in the spring of 1982—love was in the air, or maybe it was just high humidity. It was Florida, after all. I was at Disney World celebrating Grad Nite with fifty thousand of my closest friends. The end of high school was near.

"She's got to be here," I said to my best friend, Clint. We were strategically placed to watch the sea of humanity pass before us. Tom Sawyer's Island created the backdrop.

"Yeah, so is half the state of Florida," Clint responded. "You've gone to the same school as her for three years, and she doesn't know you exist."

And then, boy sees girl (for the zillionth time). I had developed a sharp eye for spotting her, seeing her float past me in the dismal high school halls. But this time, probably for the first time, girl sees boy.

At 4:00 A.M. we were all supposed to start heading back to the buses. I, not always the brightest bulb in this fluorescent world, saw my chance.

"Hey, what about one last ride on Space Mountain?"

Down through the narrow path we passed into the bowels of the "mountain", where we would get on the ride together, all the while listening to the imaginary sounds of space satellites. It set the mood for romance—although I think it was supposed to set the mood for a wild space ride.

With Lori in my lap, enveloped in my arms (for safety, I told her), love had to be in the cards. Or so I hoped. And this time, it was.

From Space Mountain we moved on to waterskiing dates on alligator-infested lakes, and our love and trust began to grow. Lake Tarpon was our ski lake of choice. It was surrounded by parkland and houses and filled with alligators (which really did not add to the allure).

Our favorite slalom ski area was a man-made canal at the end of the lake. The tall elephant grass on either side provided a perfect windbreak, giving us about a mile of waveless water in which to advance our skills (or, more importantly, show off). The canal was narrow, so the boat had to make a tight, high-speed U-turn at the end of it. The smart thing was to stay behind the boat during the turn to avoid the shore. In yet another effort to impress my future wife, I once went outside, way outside. I flew. Every muscle was tensed and flexed as I held on with one hand. *I look terrific*, I said to myself. Then I hit the shore at about sixty miles per hour and made a new path through the elephant grass and the mud. Shocked, embarrassed, and scared that I had woken a resting gator, I grabbed my ski and raced back into the lake. With mud covering my body and grass coming out my ears, I asked myself, "Could love survive such embarrassment and calamity?" It would not be the last time I would ask that question.

Gradually I learned that the feeling of love is not enough for building a lasting relationship. Feelings come and go. Feelings do not define a person; they do not dictate who he is and who he becomes. Commitments and actions are what mold a person. When it comes to marriage, the vows we make are what get us through the difficult times we are sure to experience. Keeping our vows *is* the bridge over the difficulty, and the welcome surprise is the loving feelings we find on the other side.

I had a little Hydroslide we pulled behind the boat. "Come on, Lori," I said. "I'll stand up on the Hydroslide with you sitting on my shoulders. It will be a terrific stunt. And you'll have to climb all over me." (I didn't voice that last part.)

"Are you sure?" Lori asked.

A fair question. I probably still had mud in my hair from my last fiasco.

"I got you," I answered confidently.

Why she trusted me after witnessing some of my spectacular crashes I'll never know. Maybe she had the same desire for proximity I had.

Bravely, she climbed up, and we raced across the lake. She had the scary job. The height from which she could potentially fall, coupled with the speed ... Perhaps she placed more trust in me than she should have. But her trust inspired me to be more of the man I wanted to become.

"Don't let her crash. Not too hard, anyway," I quietly prayed.

Later, the challenges and feats we would face together would require even more courage, because no amount of muscle and coordination would protect us from falling. When a successful ski pass was all we needed to accomplish in order to have a stellar day, it was easy to promise that our love for each other would remain true. After we became parents, however, that promise was put to the test.

We weren't the type to yell or throw things. Rather, in response to the stress of caring for John, we started to drift apart. Our marriage could grow with the sharing of a burden, but it could not long survive our turning away from each other. Our marriage was in trouble, not because of any huge calamity but because of our failure to take responsibility for safeguarding our relationship in small ways.

In our courting days, Lori and I wanted to know each other deeply; we wanted to support each other's dreams.

Then, at some point, we started to see more of what was lacking in each other and less of the good that was there.

My acting prospects were dimming. In my mounting frustration, I looked for more support from Lori, which I felt was in short supply. I wanted her to tell me that I was wonderful, that she believed in me. I probably didn't articulate my needs very well. Maybe I didn't even know what they were. But that didn't prevent me from blaming her for coming up short.

Meanwhile, Lori had her own needs. She pleaded with me to help more with baby John. She begged me to become a better provider somehow. And she wanted my cooperation so that she could go to Florida, alone, to be with her dying father. Her dread of losing her father was heightening her desire for security. She thought I was being selfish for not taking better care of her, and no doubt, I was. Yet I could not see a way to do any differently.

We reached the stage that most marriages arrive at sooner or later: we began to resent each other for failing to meet our expectations and for making demands we could not fulfill. We no longer saw the person we loved and admired when we got married, and we began to wonder whether we had made a terrible mistake by joining our lives together. Blinded by disappointment, we saw our dreams slipping away. We both thought we were listening to our hearts, but in fact we were listening to our fears.

And yet we managed to keep putting one foot in front of the other. Something beyond ourselves was accompanying us through this dark valley.

Lori's dad died a year and a half after his diagnosis. He worked nearly up to the end, doing his best to provide for his wife and daughters. During his final days on earth, he experienced the love of his family. We made that trip to Florida, all of us, and he felt the comfort of baby John sleeping on his big burly chest as he dozed off himself. Perhaps he was dreaming of that bright land beyond, where there are no worries and no tears.

3

# The Circle of Life

As a baby, John loved to be held, to be rocked to sleep. He seemed most comfortable when his skin was pressed against ours.

When he was a toddler, if another child took a toy away from him, he would let it go without complaint. The look on his face seemed to say, "Well, you must need it more than I do. So go ahead, take the squeaky plastic doodad. Be blessed. I'll just content myself with this soggy Cheerio I found under the couch."

John's big dimpled smile and easy laugh were the outward manifestations of a joy that glowed within. It is taking me a lifetime to discover what he had found in the first years of his life.

Thinking we had created a real masterpiece, we decided to have another child, and Benjamin was born in 1994. Lori must have taken too many vitamins or danced too much during the pregnancy, because Ben started life in overdrive and never downshifted. He loved fiercely, but pushed away when he had enough. He was funny and mischievous. Ben's world was big, and his intention was to explore every inch of it. He was an alpha dog with a fire in his belly.

Speaking of animals, as my sons were growing up, I began to imagine God as a lion. I probably began to think along these lines because I watched *The Lion King* too many times with my boys. And then The Chronicles of Narnia movies came along. I had never related to the image of God the Father as an old man with a beard. A lion is free and majestic. It moves powerfully and with grace. Old men, well, don't. I much prefer Narnia's Aslan as an image of God. He is one majestic lion. He's strong, free, wild—not safe, but good.

Yet God as a lion doesn't sit perfectly with me either. I'm more of a dog guy than a cat guy, and lions are big cats. But God as a giant dog? No, doesn't work. So, I guess I need to accept the lion symbol and stop turning on the sprinklers when the neighbor's cat steps onto my lawn. (Even though my dog and my boys think the trick is funny.)

But back to *The Lion King*. The wise monkey in the movie had to admonish Simba, the boy lion, to remember who he was. Simba ran away from his family and his responsibilities. He wanted freedom, but he used his freedom recklessly, frivolously, and in doing so, he lost himself. He forgot that he was the son of the king.

God gives us freedom, but He asks us to use it to stay close to Him so that we remember who *we* are. We are sons and daughters of the King. People, however, are like my dog. They sometimes get distracted and chase after a squirrel (or the human equivalent). And there is not a darn thing anyone can say to divert their attention back to what they are supposed to be doing, until, of course, the rodent (or whatever) has run up a tree.

We think these chases—our selfish pursuits—are so much fun. But they sometimes end in tragedy. We run in front of cars, and *splat*. We risk what is dearest to us when we follow our cloudy visions and crazy emotions.

Sometime after Ben was born, I began feeling disillusioned with my marriage. I had thought I had married my soul mate, and this proved to be a dangerous idea. The term "soul mate" can imply that there is only one perfect person to marry and that marriage with this person will be without conflict or struggle. No work, no sacrifice would be required. A lie.

Oh, how Lori and I struggled, and as a result we were letting ourselves grow apart. Of course, we both thought we were in the right. I saw her lack of interest in my career as a rejection of me. She saw my unwillingness to do something more stable as not caring for her. Our two children were not enough to keep us on the same page. We had everything—a roof over our heads, two beautiful boys, loving friends. But failing to nurture the marriage multiplied our hurt and disappointment.

When Ben was an infant, a wise older friend of mine took me for a walk. "Imagine, Joe," he said, "Saturday morning and your wife is in bed with another man. Her new husband. Then, your laughing, squealing little boys jump in with *them*, not you. Are you okay with that picture?"

A brief conversation. A vivid image. And a decision.

Right before we had nearly thrown everything away, Lori and I used our freedom wisely. We decided that even if we couldn't feel loving, we could try to treat each other with kindness, as friends, sometimes even good friends, and maybe, just maybe, all the accompanying good feelings would follow. It was the most important decision of our lives.

We didn't suddenly wake up one morning in bliss, but neither did we wake up and ask, "How did it all turn out so bad?" We just turned around and began the walk back toward each other—a few kind words, a few kind acts. Being willing to understand and to forgive.

Maybe I need to rethink my feelings toward cats. Simba may have helped to save my marriage. Or wait—maybe I should credit the wise monkey who told Simba to remember who he was. Either way, the timing was critical. We recommitted to rowing our boat together just as a storm was about to hit.

# 4

# A House, a School, and Parking

One day Lori and I were talking—dreaming—and we came to the conclusion that a house was in order. Home ownership isn't an unrealistic aspiration for most people. But most people have money when they consider making such a purchase. I did have a string of good luck and had booked a bunch of commercials, but that did not amount to a savings account.

A friend told us about a little development in Westlake Village—the suburbs. I had never heard of it. (I mean, I knew of suburbs; I just didn't know of Westlake.) It was only about thirty miles away. We took a drive, looked, and by the end of the week, we had purchased a home. Of course, we had to borrow a small fortune from a good friend for the down payment. But as we would later say, we didn't seek out Westlake; we were led there. Sure, it was far from the beach, the life-giving water, but afford-able housing near the beach was another oxymoron. This trade-off was one we would have to make.

But John had a month of kindergarten to go at Saint Monica's, and we decided to let him finish the school year there. We wanted to give him the gift of a peaceful tran-sition. He felt safe and loved at Saint Monica's, and for the most part, he colored inside the lines. So, we began driving him to school, and a friend, Dave Griffin, who had also moved to Westlake with his young family, but still worked in the Santa Monica area, pitched in to make the commute work.

Was this the beginning of a new community? God knew we would need it! In retrospect, it seemed we obeyed a calling to move to Westlake Village. The move happened so quickly. I guess God didn't need us to make plans, as He was in charge.

In our new home, we felt we had won the lottery. For the first time in our married existence, we had a driveway. Having gone without such things really makes you appreciate them. For a while, we bragged about our newfound freedom to drive to the store and back without having to spend a half hour looking for a place to park within a few blocks of home. Lori felt she was living the life of luxury with her own washer, dryer, and dishwasher—and all able to run at the same time! So this, we thought, was what living a grown-up life was all about.

Lori immediately went in search of a Catholic school for John. He longed to be in a school where he could learn his faith. In retrospect, I am convinced that John was placed on this earth to *teach* his faith. From the time he was very young, he was filled with grace and peace. We have a picture of him at age three, standing next to Lori's bedside after she gave birth to Hurricane Ben. He seems to be looking through the camera and saying to the viewer, "Everything is okay. Believe. Trust." Oh sure, he did more than his fair share of crying when he first entered this world. My mom, however, reminded me—frequently—that it wasn't near enough payback for all the crying I did during my first three years of life.

What started out as bad news—the closest Catholic school didn't have room for our son—turned into good news the day before first grade was to begin, when the school surprised Lori with a phone call: "You're not going to believe this, Mrs. Sikorra!"

A new life began to blossom: a house, a tiny yard, parking, and a budding new community. Father Dave Heney, a friend from Saint Monica's, had been transferred to the area. Wow! It all seemed a young couple's dream.

# 5

# What Do You Mean You Can't See It?

I was playing catch with John in our new front yard, preparing for his inevitable contract with the Dodgers. We
were enjoying the summer days before he began first grade
at his new school. As the ball sailed past John, he asked,
"Where is it, Daddy?"

"Right there. Right behind you."

"Where?"

*Uh-oh.*

We had his eyes checked and were promptly given a
pair of glasses.

With his new glasses and uniform, John looked as cute
as could be for his first day of school, although he felt a
bit awkward with the spectacles. At the same time, Ben
started preschool, where he too learned the importance of
coloring inside the lines, although I think he liked to learn
the rules only so he could break them with greater clarity.

John failed the eye tests administered by the school.
Then he failed the test at the pediatrician's office. "You
should go to the optometrist," the doctor said.

We were starting to feel bad about pushing John to
improve his reading. It sure is hard to read if you can't see
the letters.

The optometrist wanted John to be checked by an ophthalmologist. "His retinas don't look right," he said.

The ophthalmologist said, "Your son appears to have a deteriorating eye condition. I believe he may have some type of macular degeneration. He may lose his sight."

"How much of it?" Lori asked.

"All of it."

Blindness. How, Lori and I wondered, would we survive this?

Lori was horrified with the idea of John not being able to see the world, to take in the glory of creation that she and I appreciated so much. She was crushed. I don't think I felt horror. I think I just didn't feel. I became numb. We looked to the experts for answers, for hope. They shared only grave concern. We looked to each other. We were present. We were together (thank God). But that's about all.

Friends tried to be encouraging. "If you lose one sense, another becomes stronger," someone offered. To us, the possibility of our son developing a better sense of smell offered no consolation.

Shortly after getting this news, we went camping at beautiful McGrath State Park, on the beach in Ventura, California. John's friends, including Cameron, were running all around. John, on the other hand, kept running into things. Lori and I watched as his buddies meandered off, enjoying the freedom and fun of camping. John started to fall back. Distance. "Who would stay close to him?" we asked ourselves.

John was already legally blind when we got the initial diagnosis of macular degeneration. We felt shock—utter disbelief. We felt we had failed as parents. He was so good at compensating that we seemed to be the blind ones. He never complained of anything wrong with his eyes.

When soccer season began, we signed John up, per his desire, even though it seemed as if his eyesight worsened with each passing day. I don't think he could even see the ball. He would just follow the action as he heard it. A lot of kids at that age are pretty bad at soccer, so he didn't stick out too much. But he fumbled enough to draw some attention.

When we were told his retinas didn't look right, Lori, being in the medical field, began her own research. "If it's not just an eye disease, then it's a brain disease," she reasoned. Still, we didn't talk a lot about it with each other. We were too afraid.

We were amateurs at raising "normal" kids. How would we meet the challenge of raising a blind child? While still scratching our heads over that question, we learned that John's blindness was the least of our worries.

"Something isn't right," the ophthalmologist said. "I want him to be checked out by a geneticist."

Meanwhile, John began having night terrors. Without warning, in the middle of the night, he would begin to shriek. He would cry out and jump out of bed. Startled, we all would jump out of bed. We didn't know what was frightening him because we couldn't wake him. We couldn't comfort him. We could only try to hold him and keep him safe. The terrors would sometimes last twenty or thirty minutes, which felt like an eternity.

John hated all the doctor visits, all the tests. So did we. The poking and the prodding made him cry. The lack of good news made Lori and me cry. Everything in our lives was moving and changing so fast that we couldn't process our feelings. We were in a new home, a new community, and dealing with new medical problems. We desperately wanted someone to understand our loss, John's loss, but none of our new friends and neighbors knew our family before John's condition began to deteriorate.

After months of testing, and bottles and bottles of blood work, we got our answer at the Jules Stein Eye Institute at the University of California–Los Angeles (UCLA). Lori and I drove up to the impressive building. Its facade was a rich brown marble with tall symmetrical columns rising to the roof. Although it was a sunny day, the building seemed cold. The doctor's office was even colder. It was Ash Wednesday, February 5, 1999.

The doctor closed the door behind him after several other doctors and other medical people in white lab coats entered. I guess they were there for support. (For the doctor, I think.)

"John has juvenile neuronal ceroid lipofuscinosis," doctor number nineteen (or so it seemed) said.

"Huh?"

"Batten disease, a rare neurological degenerative disorder. Blindness is the first symptom, usually around seven years old. Kids generally develop seizures in their early teens. Then they begin to lose motor and cognitive function."

The doctor went on to explain, "At some point he will lose the ability to eat and swallow food, and even talk. He will need feeding tubes. Some kids die as early as late teens to early twenties. He may have to be institutionalized at some point. Dementia will set in, and he may be too difficult for you to handle at home."

Our minds couldn't comprehend what our ears heard. Our hearts shattered in our chests. We couldn't form words or even cogent thoughts, just tears.

"You have another child?" the doctor asked.

In halting speech we responded, "Yes. But he's fine. We're sure."

"It's genetic. One-in-four chance he has it too."

"We'll do the tests, but he's fine."

We drove across town to our old church, Saint Monica's. Ash Wednesday Mass had just begun. The church was full of worshippers for the solemn service, but we felt completely alone. We slipped into a back pew. The old Spanish Colonial church smelled powerfully of incense. We received ashes on our foreheads, a symbolic reminder of our mortality, but we had just been given that message in not so symbolic terms. The ashes seemed to cover us completely.

# 6

# Fear

John's eyesight deteriorated quickly. The teachers and staff at his school, which was not well equipped for children with disabilities, grew increasingly alarmed. Toward the end of the school year they said, "We don't think we can meet John's needs."

"We'll adjust. We can make it work."

"We think he would be better served ..."

I know the teachers and administrators felt bad as they showed us to the door, but they weren't prepared to sail into uncharted waters.

We felt rejected. Our new church and its school seemed to be letting us down in our darkest hour. In hindsight, I know that wasn't true, but fear and desperation ruled the day.

A parish, a local church, is really the people in it. And slowly, we began to experience this truth.

As our first Halloween after the Batten diagnosis approached, Lori's eyes welled up with tears. She did not know how we should manage the situation. Of course we could take John trick-or-treating, but how was he to experience the simple childhood pleasure of running from door to door? Was he to be denied that sense of freedom?

We met Alison Kale and her family through Ben's preschool, and we invited them to go trick-or-treating with us in our neighborhood. Without prompting, Alison, who was John's age, gently wrapped her hand in his. Dressed up as Cleopatra, with a pound of eyeliner for a not-so-subtle accent, she was super excited. (Her excitement over life's little pleasures never wavered over the years.) She and Ninja John made a perfect couple. Gently, she led him from door to door, and they began gathering the coveted Snickers bars for me—I mean for themselves. Theirs was a relationship born in simple acceptance and bad costumes, but it lasted a lifetime. Ben lustily led the attack, fleecing the neighbors before *and* after John and Alison arrived at the door. He was also dressed up as a ninja. I guess we weren't the most creative parents.

In our short time in this new community, the people, God's people, began to open their hearts to us. Families we barely knew began to encircle us, enveloping us with love. Still reeling from the shock of the diagnosis, Lori and I probably didn't fully appreciate the love they offered. Even when we did feel the appropriate amount of gratitude, we also felt that we were not giving enough in return for the generosity. Let's just say that these new relationships were difficult for us. Clearly we had entered into a stage of life that required resilience if we were to survive; and resilience, I was beginning to learn, meant not only relying on one's own strength but also recognizing and accepting help. No, we couldn't just lie down and die (although we sometimes felt as though we wanted to do just that).

I wanted to talk meaningfully to John about the diagnosis and the way the disease would progress, but I didn't know what to say. For one thing, I didn't understand the disease myself. For example, the doctors said he would eventually have dementia. In my early thirties, I didn't even know how to spell the word, much less what the condition looked like. The doctors also said he would lose motor control, and I didn't know anything about feeding tubes and the other devices that assist those who can no longer do ordinary things for themselves. So, what was I supposed to tell John? How was I to help him to understand what was happening to him, and what was going to happen?

Another reason I didn't know what to say to John was that I had no vision for John's future or my own as his father. No medical professional spoke to us of joy or laughter or fullness of life in spite of the challenges. Not meaning to, they outlined only burdens and losses. High school, college, career, marriage, children—these would not be in John's future, and I would not be able to enjoy them vicariously as the proud father or the fulfilled grandfather. In an instant, I was deprived of the dreams a father has for his son. If I were to find a path ahead for us, I would have to look for it in a place I had never looked before.

John, meanwhile, refused to stop living. As his eyesight diminished, he bravely insisted on riding, running, and doing all the other things a boy wants to do. After crashing into a pole or another object, he would stand up, rub his head, and ask, "Where did that come from?"

He worked hard at trying to remember where he had put things so that he could find them later. When he couldn't remember, he would patiently grope around, searching the floor or his toy box for the missing item. When he came up empty-handed, Ben would race in to help.

"Here, John. Here it is."

Later, though, when he was secured comfortably in his bed or in our arms, John's tears, born out of frustration and sadness, would flow. The tears gave voice to his pain over the realization that everything before his eyes was fading into gray. Lori and I struggled to offer words of support, but sadly they gave little consolation.

I wanted to be a hero for my family, but I too felt so broken. Perhaps that was the perfect place for us to meet— the place where all our brokenness was laid bare. Connect. Touch. Hold. That's what John taught us. We would hold him, and each other, tighter.

Later, Ben would find us. Trying to escape the pain he felt, he would say, "I don't want to hear John cry anymore." And then we would realize that Ben needed just as much of our support and encouragement as John. Ben had hope, though. "Maybe when John is older, he won't need me so much," he would say.

My family's pain crippled me. My pain crippled me. I wanted to keep moving forward, but I didn't know how. Yet not moving meant giving in to depression and death of the soul. So I took one step at a time. Just one step.

In one of the *Star Trek* movies, when Captain Kirk was asked for a heading, he replied, "Out there." Out there lies the unknown, which the *Enterprise* was built to explore. The spaceship can't stay parked at the dock. Its whole purpose is to go "out there". And its crew signed up for the adventure and the danger of going along for the ride. My family was on the *Enterprise*, I realized. Maybe every family is, and John's illness simply gave us the gift of knowing it. Our spaceship's warp drive did not seem to be working, however, so the pace of our discoveries was going to be on the slow side.

We had always prayed as a family, and we had tried to nurture in the boys a loving relationship with God. We frequently spoke of heaven and the blessings yet to come, while trying to experience all the blessings God gives us in the here and now, which point toward Him. One night, following prayer time, John asked Lori, "Mommy when

you die and come back to be my angel, will you promise
not to be invisible? I want to know you are there."

With tears in her eyes she responded, "I will always be
here, John. You will know. You will feel me."

Our job, here and now, is to make love visible.

And our friends at Saint Monica's did just that. They
started a fund to support our family's needs—whatever
they might be. They had yard sales, put on plays, and held
concerts. God's people, strangers and friends alike, stepped
up to the plate.

Yet this outpouring of generosity also brought some pain.

One friend said to my wife, "You don't know, Lori.
People have given until it hurts. And you don't know
what that feels like."

"I don't know what it feels like?"

Silence.

"I don't know?"

"I need to take a break from this friendship."

"Please. Take it all back. I don't understand," Lori said.
But the friend was no longer listening. She had reached
her limit.

The loss of the friendship was devastating, and the timing was terrible. Years later, Lori explained it this way:
"Our frying pan was heating up, and not everyone was
going to jump in."

Understandable, but still painful. That's how it can be in
the Body of Christ, in which people are still people. They are
trying, with God's grace, to love, to give. But they have
limits. We all do.

With time we came to see that our lives are really a
beautiful symphony conducted by God. Different instruments enter the piece at different times. When some
instruments fall silent, other wonderful ones enter, and the
symphony continues to move, to build, to grow. With

that insight, we could let go of the fear of being too much of a burden on any one person and then being hurt and disappointed when a person pulled back. Thus, Lori was able to forgive, to let go of the hurts, to trust in God. And doing that is what opens the door for reconciliation and personal growth.

If all the instruments played the same thing simultaneously, it would sound like me and Ben having one of our rare band practices, using all our more vibrant (read "loud") instruments, with the amps cranked to overload, while we worked on our newest extemporaneously created tune called "Noise".

Slowly we were learning that God has something more beautiful than noise in mind for us.

# 7

# Meet the Enemy, but Not Alone

The summer following the diagnosis, Lori and I flew to the annual Batten conference in Chicago to meet our adversary face-to-face. By far, it was the most difficult confrontation ever.

At the conference were other parents of children with Batten disease and brainiac doctors who study mice and flies in search of cures for diseases. Despite the image of them as weird scientists with inch-thick glasses, these experts were very human and very compassionate. That discovery was the good news. But from the beginning of our stay in Chicago, we had to hear the bad news too.

At O'Hare Airport, as we were boarding the hotel van, we saw a child with Batten disease. He was reclining in a wheelchair, with arms and legs drawn up into a fetal position, drooling, and making guttural sounds. His beautiful eyes stared blankly, seeing nothing. Looking at this child, we didn't see someone's beautiful son; we saw our own dark future. During the drive to the hotel, I fought every impulse to hijack the van and turn it back to the airport. I wasn't ready to move forward, if this was forward; I wanted to escape. But we pressed ahead.

Entering the hotel lobby, we saw other kids, some walking with canes, some being carried. Wordlessly, we checked in. We wanted to close our eyes, ears, and hearts.

We crawled to our room and collapsed on our bed, sobbing. "Not us. Not our son. This can't be true," we said to each other.

But we had come for information and signs of hope. We couldn't remain closed off and locked away.

The next day, bleary-eyed from tears and lack of sleep, we attended our first lecture. We were given information, but not the hope we longed for.

"We've finally identified the defective gene," the doctors said.

"What? That's it?"

Throughout the weekend, we listened for words such as "cure". Although the possibility of a cure was talked about, reality hit hard: no cure was likely to be discovered in our son's lifetime.

At the conference, we realized we were being naïve, living in denial. We met many families who had more than one child affected with Batten disease, and upon our return, we promised, we would get Ben tested. Yet he wouldn't have to go through all that John had, we reassured ourselves. We *knew* he was okay.

After the conference, we knew that our lives would be radically altered by John's disease. Our immediate future was going to be even more different from what we had anticipated. For one thing, we didn't come away from the conference with any knowledge that could stop or slow the advance of the disease. We remained in touch with some of the doctors we met, and even befriended some of them, but they could do only so much. Although we didn't abandon all hope for a miracle of science, we knew that our best hope would be a miracle from God. Yes, we would continue to do all that could be medically done for John. But letting go and trusting God was the only real way to go.

Several years before we married, while Lori still lived in Florida and I in New York, during one of my frequent trips back home we walked to our favorite dock on the bay. (Really, it's not just a song.) We watched yet another spectacular Florida sunset light up the sky with deep purples, reds, and yellows. Letting out a thoughtful sigh I said, "It may be difficult for you to deal with my inevitable fame." (Okay, that wasn't one of my deeper insights.)

Later, however, the conversation became a little more prophetic, a bit more somber and tender. We began talking about having kids.

"What if we had disabled children?" Lori asked.

Perhaps two young lovers talking about having kids isn't too unusual. Yet how often do they discuss having less-than-perfect kids? It's easy to imagine a cute little munchkin sitting in a high chair with food in his hair, and perhaps to imagine how we might have to talk him through the inevitable sadness following the loss of a Little League game. But disability?

We didn't have the words, the life experience, or the maturity to expand on the imaginings of our hearts and minds, but the love that was growing between us seemed to form a mysterious bond that would be the fabric holding us together when life became difficult.

"We would be okay," we decided. How or why we came to that conclusion I do not know. Was it because we were sitting in the magnificence of God's creation, witnessing a majestic sunset? Or because we were seeing life through the eyes of young love that knows only faith in the happiness that lies ahead? Was it grace? Revelation? Was it possible that the God of the universe cared enough to let us in on His plan? I know only that seeds of trust were being planted.

We did not have this conversation again until years later, when we were faced with the enormity of John's diagnosis and it seemed as if a prophecy had been fulfilled, as if God had indeed begun to prepare our hearts when they were still green. We reflected on that conversation before we were married, when we talked about having a disabled child.

And we began to see the wisdom in the words of Lori's father. On our wedding day, as Lori prepared to walk down the aisle, fear began creeping up her spine. She turned to her father and asked, "How do you do this, this marriage thing, for the rest of your life?"

"You don't," he said. "You just do it today. Then tomorrow you do it again. And before you know it, you've done it for a lifetime."

Advice from heaven, through the lips of an old, hard-working tool and die maker. Our biggest fear, we realized, was not of the difficult tasks set before us today, but of the harder ones that the future might bring. Fear comes from our vain attempt to live in the future, but peace is found in the moment.

Such is the case for every one of us, with or without disabled children. Fear of the future is one of the biggest stressors, one of the biggest causes of insomnia and depression. Yet none of us knows the future, and worrying about it is useless—worse than that: it is destructive.

Lori and I figured that the only way to conquer our fear of the future was to embrace the present, which is, after all, the only thing we really have, and to live life to the fullest right now. With this resolve, we decided to make a second trip that summer (and to pay for it with an already extended credit card). We went to North Carolina, where my large family gathered together at Lake Fontana, with its hundreds of miles of shoreline surrounded by mountains and trees. We went there for the kind of support that only family can give. We went to laugh and to play in the great outdoors.

I grew up the youngest of eight kids (six boys and two girls) and was sometimes referred to as the runt of the litter. My nickname was Peanut. Even though I was small, somehow I never felt small, nor did I think small. In a large family, a child needs to toughen up and to stand up for himself, or he gets beat up until he fades into the background.

When I was seven, my family moved from Minnesota to Florida. We moved into a big house on a dead-end street, although nothing feels big when occupied by so many boisterous children. The size of the house didn't really matter, though, because we spent the majority of our time outside or on the big screened-in porch on the shady side of the house. On hot days, when the temperature reached into the 90s, with nearly 100 percent humidity (it only seemed as if it were 112 degrees), that porch was our favorite place to watch the thunderstorms roll in and to hang out together until late into the night. (Actually, our mom always made us go to bed when she did—a habit she never broke even when we became adults. She couldn't bear to miss out on any excitement or good conversation.)

After Mom fed us, she pushed us outdoors. Usually I would leave the house in the morning barefoot and return only when hungry. I explored storm drains under our town and woods that no longer exist; I opened my life to adventure.

When I was about twelve, I had a formative experience with a bully. I was riding my bike toward a bridge spanning the Intracoastal Waterway, which leads to the Gulf of Mexico. Some young guy, already working at covering his muscles with a layer of fat and holding a fishing pole, refused to let me pass. Using the skills I had developed to avoid getting beat up by one of my brothers, I talked my way around him.

"Come back this way, and I'll throw you and your bike off the bridge," he snarled.

An unpleasant prospect, as the bridge was high, the current swift, and the water full of sharks.

I reached the other side of the bridge and stewed. Then I turned around and headed back toward my aggressor. I was scared, but something deeper, stronger, led me back to confront the man—and my own fear. Foolish or not, I was ready to pit my sinewy hundred pounds of flesh and resolve against him. Maybe I wasn't thinking clearly. Or maybe I never had such clarity in my life.

I could tell he was surprised to see me, but he was silent. After a few tense moments (maybe we were both hoping a fish would bite), I simply moved his fishing equipment and rode by. No doubt, I acted cooler than I felt. As I recall this story, I see where my son Ben got his innate disdain for bullies.

Whenever I get together with my brothers and sisters, and we share our childhood adventures, we marvel that any of us survived to adulthood. Our stories require very little embellishment to sound harrowing and fun at the same time because our experiences were harrowing and fun. Surely our mother's unceasing prayers kept us all alive.

We were raised devout Catholics. Every weekend, the ten of us would file into church and take up an entire pew. I received my faith in the lap of comfort and the love of family. Later, my faith matured in the school of pain and the fire of adversity, but it was my family who had given me the foundation of trust that I needed to grow through those challenges. Is it any wonder, then, that when Lori and I needed support during that summer of 1999, we went to the family gathering in North Carolina?

We bought John and Ben a pair of small beginner water skis painted white. John couldn't see well enough for us to teach him how to ski using visual cues; he would need to learn by feeling the experience. We both put on skis, and I put John in front of me so that I would be able to help him stand up as the boat accelerated. I put my skis outside his to prevent his from drifting apart. Perfect plan, except when the boat took off, his skis fell right off his little feet. I wrapped him in one arm and held on to the rope with the other. He beamed and the family cheered. His first time up, and already he was doing tricks—his feet dangling in the air and sometimes splashing in the water. He smiled and waved toward the sound of the cheers. A star was born.

"Barefoot skiing!" we shouted. "It usually takes years of practice before you can ski barefoot."

Perhaps John's first experience of waterskiing is a metaphor for our relationship with God. He lifts us up so that we can enjoy the ride He wants to give us. We need only beam, wave, and give thanks that someone is holding us. Of course, it helps if we hold on too, and follow directions.

I'll-Do-It-My-Way-Ben decided he had seen enough to know he wasn't going to learn to ski that day. It is sometimes what we see that causes us fear, while simple trust allows us to take risks. Ben felt completely victorious, however, when he tubed behind the boat later that afternoon.

We had a great adventure that week—skiing, whitewater rafting down cold mountain rivers, eating wonderful barbecue while looking out over the tranquil lake. Even more important, we connected as a family. We began to share our story, our journey, but with very few words. We didn't talk a lot about the disease. And no one tried to make it all better. It was enough to drink in the blessing of being in the presence of love.

As a family, Lori and I realized, we would need to define ourselves by the goodness we could experience, not by what we would be missing.

## 8

# Life Becomes Tougher

The perfect storm was building, and the shelter was faltering. Nearly all my commercials that had been running on television tanked at once, and so did the money—not to mention the health insurance that was tied to my income. Lori, understandably, was freaking out, not just because of the money but because of the confluence of struggles. I can't say I was doing better.

Lori had been working part-time as a nurse and full-time as a mommy. Although I had gotten a lot better at carrying my part of the parenting load, she still did the heavy lifting. Caring for small children is difficult. And for the most part, our mornings and evenings probably looked a lot like those of other parents raising young kids. But our son's deteriorating condition and the knowledge that he might live only a few short years made our job even harder. Finally, Lori hit a wall.

"I can't work. I can't take care of these very sick people at work when I don't even know how to take care of my own son," she said. She needed to pull back and stay home with the boys.

Who could blame her? Neither of us knew how to take proper care of John. Our feeling of helplessness was devastating, and we felt mostly alone in our anguish.

For many of life's tough problems we don't have to look far to find answers.

"My marriage is in crisis."

"Here are the names of fifteen marriage therapists within a mile of your home."

"I need a better job."

"Here are the want ads."

"I'm hungry."

"The store is down the block, and the shelves are full."

"My son has been diagnosed with a rare, incurable disease that nobody's ever heard of. His eyesight is diminishing quickly, and his cognitive skills are waning. We've been told that eventually his condition will be so extreme that he will likely need institutional care."

Silence.

Lori and I shared many dreams, but our dominant desire at that moment was to flee. We wanted to escape with our boys to a deserted island where we could live out the time we were given. We didn't know anyone near us who could share our experience, and God knows, we wouldn't want anyone to share our experience. There were only a couple of hundred kids in the country with Batten disease.

My faith was shaken, challenged as never before. Any stock I had placed in achieving financial stability from my acting career was gone. The appearance of health, I realized, was an illusion. Or rather, good health could not be expected to last—it too could vanish in a puff of smoke. The hard truth, among many hard truths, was that it was time for me to let go of my dreams: dreams of healthy kids with bright futures; dreams of fulfilling careers.

Increasingly I was feeling like a failure, unable to stay ahead of the bills with my chosen profession, unable to keep my son free from harm, unable to give my wife the time with the children that she and they needed. As much as I loved acting, I knew more deeply than ever before that my first and foremost duty—and desire—was to take care of my family. My truest fulfillment would be realized by doing that, which meant I needed to find another livelihood.

By this time, I had received my bachelor's degree from UCLA. The problem was that it was in theater, which qualified me to, well, act as if I knew how to do something. The only other ace in my hand was my connection with the police department. I was fortunate to be a known quantity there. My years as a reserve police officer had earned me a good reputation and made me a safe hire.

Yet, selfishly, I was scared to death of becoming a professional cop. The risk that frightened me was not of suffering physical harm but of losing my voice, my creative voice. From childhood I had cultivated this voice, beginning in the kitchen, where I would sing and bang pots and pans with my brothers and sisters as we washed dishes together. My singing in the kitchen evolved into singing in the church choir (although the choir directors didn't approve of pots and pans). Next I discovered acting in local theatrical productions, and then I began booking national commercials while still in high school.

"Okay, Joe, for this audition you have to act like a monkey."

"Are you kidding? I'm gonna give you a nine-hundred-pound gorilla!"

Getting paid for acting like the goofball I already was had seemed a pretty sweet gig. I think I could have coined the phrase "money for nothing and chicks for free" if Dire Straits hadn't sung it first.

No doubt, acting gave me the attention I had learned to enjoy in my youth. Best of all, it fueled my active imagination. I loved to create, to dream. I had always dreamed big. And for the most part, I was bold enough (sometimes foolish enough) to take the necessary steps to pursue making my dreams reality.

Music too fueled my creative side. When I was about twelve, I took piano lessons. I was undisciplined and rarely practiced. I mostly faked my way through, playing by ear while staring at the sheet music. Really, piano lessons were just another chance to use my acting chops. My teacher, Mrs. Noise (no kidding), didn't push me very hard. Instead she encouraged me to find my own song. Years later, when I began to write music, I blessed her and cursed her (mostly blessed her). It would have been nice to have known how to read music, but I really can blame no one but myself for not studying musical notation when I had the chance.

Given that I had been performing for my whole life and that my gifts had thrived in freedom, I was afraid of what being a professional cop might do to me. I would be entering a regimented world, with lots of regulations and red tape. Would I suffocate in such an environment? Would I lose my creative edge?

One of the things I treasured about being an actor was the ability to tell stories, and I feared losing that art. But what if I was being called to be part of a story that God was telling? What if I was being asked not to act a part but to live one? And what if the story God wanted to tell with my life, with my family, would contain all the best elements of any great story—sacrifice, death, and redemption?

But there was a catch. To say yes to being part of God's story, I would need to let go of the story I had been creating for myself. With time and maturity, I eventually learned that my purpose is not to fulfill the dream I had for my life but to pour myself out for others. Acting was fun and rewarding, but it did not make me a better person and could not, therefore, make me truly happy. I would find myself, become a better me, and be fulfilled as a person only as I gave myself to others—particularly my family.

I was hired as a full-time employee at the Santa Monica Police Department on August 23, 1999, and I was paid to attend another police academy, which required me to live away from home for six months. The time apart was going to be tough on the whole family. We wanted to huddle together for warmth, to experience the reassurance of physical closeness and affection. But knowing that my becoming a full-time police officer was the right thing for all of us would see us through the pain of separation.

Like a man in the military leaving for a deployment, I packed my gear and shaved my head. Flooded with emotion, I held my little boys, kissed my wife, and drove away. Silently. I wanted to be with my family more than anything in the world. Time was incredibly precious. But if I couldn't be with them, I could live my life for them.

After I had been in the academy for several brutal months, Lori met me at my apartment door. Her expression was pained.

"Ben's got it," she said. "He has Batten's too."

We collapsed into each other's arms. If we said anything to each other, I don't remember what it was. We went to a nearby restaurant and stared at our food growing cold for about an hour before driving home.

As we had promised the doctors at the conference in Chicago, we had taken Ben for testing a few weeks earlier. We weren't kept waiting long for the news we never wanted—never expected.

I took the next day off. It was all the time the police force could give me, but not nearly enough for us to process the enormity of our pain. That would take a lifetime.

On February 23, 2000, I was sworn in as a full-time police officer. Instead of elation, I felt numbness. Lori and I were simply going through the motions of fulfilling our responsibilities, the way people do after the death of a loved one. Bereavement probably best describes the state we were in. We were grieving for our sons, even though they were still living, and the family life we would never have. All the progress we seemed to have made in accepting John's illness, in living joyfully in the moment, was washed away by the tidal wave of Ben's diagnosis.

After the loss of his wealth, his children, and his health, Job, the ultimate sufferer of the Old Testament, was in a similar state when his wife gave him some bad advice: "Curse God and die, Job."

Neither Lori nor I cursed God (which is really a dumb and possibly dangerous thing to do), but we did feel as if we wanted to die.

Job's friends tried to "console" him by "helping" him to see the error of his ways. According to their logic, since God punishes the sinful and rewards the good, Job must have sinned terribly for God to be punishing him so severely. "Get right with God," they told him. "You know bad things don't happen to good people, so fess up." But Job was convinced of his own righteousness.

By no means was I convinced of my righteousness. I had made all kinds of mistakes in my life. So I thought it was my fault that my kids were sick and my wife was sad. I bought into the explanations of Job's friends, and as a consequence, I carried terrible guilt for years. I might have avoided this unnecessary guilt if I had understood the message of the book of Job. In the end, God gives Job and his foolish friends a comeuppance: "Who is this that darkens counsel by words without knowledge?" (Job 38:2). Then the Lord asks Job:

Where were you when I laid the foundation of the earth?
   Tell me, if you have understanding.
Who determined its measurements—surely you know!
   Or who stretched the line upon it?
On what were its bases sunk,
   or who laid its cornerstone,
when the morning stars sang together,
   and all the sons of God shouted for joy?
Or who shut in the sea with doors,
   when it burst forth from the womb;
when I made clouds its garment,
   and thick darkness its swaddling band,
and prescribed bounds for it.

(Job 38:4–10)

In other words, we mere mortals are not wise enough to understand the ways of God, the Creator of the universe, who is so far above us. "Enter into the mystery" is what God was saying to Job. "You'll find me there and more and better life besides." If I had understood this back in 2000, I might not have believed that my family's suffering was my fault.

As best we could, Lori and I turned toward each other. Somehow, we needed to learn how to let go of even more of what we had wanted for our lives and to begin the long, difficult path of trying to embrace what God had in store for us. There was grace enough for each day, no more, no less, like manna in the desert. And like God's people wandering in the wilderness, one day at a time, we too needed to choose life, with deliberation, at every turn.

A good friend of mine, an actor named Clint Carmichael, asked me, "What now, Joe? What are you going to do?"

"Find my way back to the water."

# 9

# Choosing Life

John had some pretty tough emotional times trying to adapt to his losses. He smiled and laughed but often felt lonely. Through tears he would ask us over and over why he couldn't see. Most days, however, his indomitable spirit continued to prevail. Ben, at age five, didn't have any symptoms of the disease. He was wild, but that was just Ben.

We found VIP (Very Important Player) soccer and baseball programs, which accommodate kids with special needs. With the assistance of a sighted player who led him into the action, John scored numerous goals. With only a count of "One, two, three, swing!" he hit pitched baseballs into the outfield. The rules were few, but the satisfaction of play was great!

One might expect the helper kids to look bored and irritated while helping children like John, but they were just the opposite. They were as enthusiastic about the play as the kids they were helping. And forget about rude, angry parents in the stands. The parents cheered wildly—for every kid, for both teams. There was definitely something to be learned from these games.

John also studied and competed in karate. Clearly, he couldn't spar on the open mat with the other kids, but he competed in foot sweeping and grappling. And on Sundays, he sang in the church's children's choir.

While he struggled, learned, and grew, he continued to teach us about God's abundant love. At prayer time one night, Ben asked Lori why she had been crying at a healing service they had attended.

Lori couldn't find the words, but John had an answer: "Mommy may cry, but Jesus cries the most. He hears our pain and wants to take it all away." He continued, saying, "Jesus cries the most on Sundays because that's when most people pray."

Though faith had always played a role in Lori's life, she hadn't always been Catholic. When we married in 1987, the ceremony was performed by Lori's Southern Baptist minister and my Catholic priest. Needless to say, it was a challenge to decide how much alcohol could be served at the reception. My family questioned whether the marriage could be considered consummated without some dancing on the tables while drinking adult libations, and Lori's family was pretty sure that she had been led seriously astray.

Before the big event, we were counseled by both ministers, Father Tom and Brother Bill.

"Joe," Brother Bill said in his wonderful Southern drawl, "I'd love to see you become Baptist, but it seems your Catholic faith is pretty strong."

At that time, Lori and I were comfortable sharing our faith together and felt at home in any church we attended. But when we had kids, Brother Bill advised us, we would run into difficulties. "You want to go to one church, and your spouse the other—the kids will exploit the difference, and you'll lose the church experience altogether. You guys need to get together on this."

Four years into the marriage, Lori, taking her pastor's advice, converted to Catholicism. Her grandmother turned over in her grave, and the Sikorras began a new journey in our faith, one that wasn't based on piety alone, but also great meals and celebration of life—even at the worst of times.

Shortly after John's diagnosis, we began the practice of laying our hands on each other for healing: on Lori's heart for much needed patience, on Ben's head for obedience (always needed), and on John's eyes for sight. When the family put their hands on me, John would sigh. Tell me he didn't have vision!

Ben began giving prekindergarten a whirl. Some days, Lori didn't even have to stay. (She thought her school days were over.) Lori tried to get him excited about school, saying he would meet a lot of kids. He told her he didn't need new friends; all he needed was her. Those words bought a lot of forgiveness and made a substantial deposit in the patience bank account.

Mostly, Ben was content playing at home with John and the neighborhood kids. He enjoyed playing basketball, riding his scooter, and roller-skating with one skate and one tennis shoe. (I guess he liked to stay somewhat grounded.) We were incredibly proud of him and his natural willingness to help John when needed, offering a hand to lead him in the right direction or helping to find a lost toy.

Because of the generosity of friends who held fundraisers, we were able to provide some incredible experiences for the boys and create some wonderful memories. We camped in Yosemite in the spring and water-skied in the summer. Lori's sister, Suzi, and her husband, John, treated us to a trip to Colorado, where they had an adaptive snow-ski program. Ben and his cousin Travis skied, and John kept up with the benefit of a sighted guide calling out, "Left, left, left, right, right, right, stop! stop! stop!!!" Of course, he wasn't satisfied with "just" skiing. He convinced his guide to take him down the racecourse.

Fueled by adventure, equipped with courage, and guided by a shared ski pole, they took off. Faster and faster, they swooshed down the mountain until the "agony of defeat" moment. Everyone watching gasped as the plume of snow signaled the crash. Slowly, the dynamic duo rose to their feet (absent skis) and waved. No agony. No defeat. Just the thrill of living life. All that distinguished John from a snowman was that his huge smile revealed teeth, not coal.

We vowed to remain active for as long as possible. "Adapt" became the key word to staying in the flow of life. We knew life would eventually slow us down, but it would have to catch us first!

# 10

# Healing and Suffering

Our family motto became *Carpe diem* (Seize the day)—
except for on Friday nights, when it became *Carpe victus*,
which is roughly translated "Seize the food." (More about
that later.)

We committed to living each day fully, with as much
joy and laughter as possible. Even Scripture says cheer-
fulness is good medicine (cf. Prov 17:22). It's easy to find
things that make you sad or angry. Just turn on the news.
What's less frequently reported are the things that make
you laugh or that inspire feelings of gratitude. In our family, we became really good at finding the humor in life.

When John's disabilities forced him to leave his Catholic grade school, he was full of personality, but he needed
a full-time aide to help him navigate around the school.
He was strong, nimble, and athletic, but he was beginning to suffer mild mental impairments. His short-term
memory was faltering, making learning more difficult. A
year or so later, we still felt sad about his not being able
to attend the school that had meant so much to him.
Although our minds understood the situation, our hearts
still needed healing.

One day when I was feeling irritable, the phone rang,
and I hoped it was someone selling something I didn't need.

Whenever I had a salesperson on the line, I would do my best to irritate him by telling him a very long, tedious story about my day: "You see, when I got up this morning at 7:37—I normally get up at 7:35, but this morning felt different ..." That mischief would have to wait, however, as the caller turned out to be the pastor of the church whose school we had been asked to leave. "I have some friends who are affiliated with the Knights of Malta," the priest said.

*Hey*, I thought, *this could be cool.* I had no clue who the Knights of Malta were, but I knew that knights were medieval noble warriors with horses, helmets, and swords.

"Long story short," the pastor continued, "they'd like to sponsor your family to go to Lourdes, France."

Perhaps we weren't the only ones who felt bad about our having to leave the school. The pastor was reaching out, trying to do what he could. I was grateful, and my heart softened with the gesture.

"Talk to me, Father."

"There have been many miracles there," the priest explained. "This is part of what the Knights do. They take people there, pray, and ..."

It didn't sound as if we would witness any battles. But I found out later that the Knights of Malta had fought some epic ones, defending Christendom from Muslim invaders. They also founded hospitals, and today their main mission is to care for the sick. Their motto is *Tuitio fidei et obsequium pauperum* (Defense of the faith and service to the poor).

Lori and I decided to accept the Knights' generous offer. Time away as a family to pray, to be with people who cared, whose mission is to reach out to the sick and disabled and to bring them into a deeper relationship with the Lord—it sounded wonderful.

"We'd love to go," I said. "We have become very open to miracles."

Of course, there were some significant obstacles, such as my new police job. I was out of the academy, but I had only just finished my field training. I had no vacation time, and no one expected a rookie to be asking for time off at this point. I went to my boss.

"Lieutenant, we've been given this opportunity."

"I think we can make it happen, Joe." First Lourdes miracle.

Once in Lourdes, we prayed a lot, which is what you are supposed to do on *pilgrimages*, I now understand. I immediately had to dismiss any notion that we were going to try to take back a city. That's what you do on *crusades*. (I have to stop watching so many action movies.)

Lourdes is a small town in the foothills of the Pyrenees. It was made famous when Mary, the Mother of Jesus, appeared in a grotto, a cave being used as a pigsty, to a sickly girl named Bernadette. Bernadette and her family lived in abject poverty, but they had deep love and devotion for each other, and deep faith. How often, it seems, God chooses the lowly, the poor, and the obscure places to reveal heaven's blessings.

Although miraculous healings have occurred at the spring that Mary revealed to Bernadette, the girl herself was told by Mary, "I do not promise to make you happy in this world, but in the next." Bernadette lived with suffering her whole life and died a painful death at the age of thirty-five. Here was a message for me: think eternity. I wasn't ready to hear it, however.

In spite of all of the hotels and the shops that cater to pious visitors, Lourdes is incredibly beautiful, surrounded by deep-green mountains. A fast-flowing river, the Gave de Pau, runs through the city, which is home to about fifteen thousand residents and is visited by about five million pilgrims each year.

Mary told Bernadette to ask that a chapel be built by the grotto and to invite people to come there in procession, to pray, and to wash in the spring. A beautiful basilica sits above the grotto, and nearby are baths where pilgrims take turns plunging into the healing water. The pilgrims process to the baths, where they are ceremoniously led into the washbasin and, wearing nothing but white robes or towels, are submerged in the cold spring water.

The word for "procession" in the dialect of the region means a pilgrimage outside one's parish in order to meet with the People of God on their journey through life. This concept became a healing force in our family. Meeting with others on their journeys renewed our strength and courage.

While processing to the pools, Ben discovered he would have to take off his clothes. He was only five years old, but he made it clear that he was not going to submit to the ordeal. Instead, as he passed the fountains where pilgrims could drink the spring water or fill bottles with it, he doused himself with water. Ben believed in the power of God to heal him, but God had given him a stout heart; and he wasn't going to be told what he had to do to be healed. He said very emphatically that he had taken his "Jesus bath" at the fountain.

We passed the beautiful church and the grotto as we approached the baths. As we wound our way back and forth through the line to enter the structure with the baths, we felt a bit as though we were at Disneyland. It wasn't a magic kingdom we were seeking, however, but majesty and mystery and a deeper connection with God—a God who could heal, who wanted to heal. The question was: How would He choose to manifest healing in our lives? We didn't know.

We saw crutches hung on the walls, evidence of healings. We all felt a little excited at the possibilities, but we also remembered the message to Bernadette: "Not in this life ..."

There are two sets of baths, one for men and another for women. Some very sick people were being carried on gurneys by volunteers; many others were in wheelchairs. Inside, volunteers from all over the world helped us to undress and then wrapped us in a towel. Lori said she initially felt a bit uncomfortable undressing, but then she realized that the volunteers seemed not even to notice her body. They were consumed with prayer as they led us down the stone steps and into the giant tubs. Reverently, they prayed while giving us the opportunity to offer up our intentions silently. It was humbling and powerful as these strangers enveloped us with their care. We felt covered in love even before being submerged in the ten-foot-long tub.

Ben watched Lori as she was gently laid back into the water. But nothing he saw changed his mind about having already taken his "Jesus bath". In another room, John and I both let ourselves be dipped into the cold water.

The experience was deeply moving. There were no sudden cures, but perhaps we were blessed in the same way as Bernadette: given the grace to grow in deep love and devotion through suffering.

The pilgrimage made me look more deeply at my own belief in miracles. Pilgrims travel to Lourdes to be healed, and there have been countless claims of healing, both physical and spiritual. Sixty-nine of the physical cures have been studied by medical doctors who found them to be without natural explanation, thus miraculous. Yet Bernadette herself suffered greatly and died young. Here is another mystery I do not claim to understand.

All along our pilgrimage, we found love—for each other, our family, and our community. And the evident growth of that love kept us from sinking beneath the heavy weight we carried. Was this inner transformation a miracle? Yes, I believe it was.

Lori was given an additional sign. She would confess to being the Doubting Thomas of the family, and she desperately wanted to quell her doubts. She needed to know that heaven was real, and that if her children suffered and died from Batten disease she would see them in heaven healed and whole.

"I need to know, Lord. I need to know," she fervently prayed.

Upon our return, we met with friends who had been praying the Rosary for us. They promised to pray for us each day we were in Lourdes. Lori's friend Kerry explained that on the first night of their prayer vigil, her rosary chain turned gold. She gave that rosary to Lori.

"I'm real, Lori. Heaven is real," God seemed to be saying by this sign.

Lori kept and treasured the gift for many years, until she gave it to her friend Heidi, who was the boys' first soccer coach in the VIP program and had brought organized play back into their lives when it didn't seem possible. She was a wife and a mother of three young boys, and she was dying of cancer. After a long battle, she succumbed to the disease in 2009. But she died with the assurance and the peace of knowing she was going to heaven. After she died, Lori asked the family if they still had the rosary. It was not to be found.

The chain's turning gold was not the first amazing thing we had experienced in our lives. Many gifts and blessings along the way could be seen as miracles, or they could be seen in a cynical way, as coincidences, as events that would have turned out well whether we had prayed or not, as occurrences with a natural explanation.

Such reasoning is beside the point. It's all gift—our lives and everything that happens to us. And when I see my life in this way, and give thanks for it, my heart is lighter.

Leading up to and following our visit to Lourdes, our new community grew in love and support. Friends performed so many acts of kindness: a backpack full of Ben's favorite things for the long trip; a year of housekeeping service for Lori to reduce her workload; various fund-raising events. An engaged couple even asked for donations to support John's and Ben's upcoming needs in lieu of wedding gifts. Each time we thought or spoke of a concern, a need, or a desire, God provided.

I was continuously challenged to grow beyond myself, to allow God to provide what I could not, to be humbled and to allow others to give what I could not, and to learn to hold the things of this world loosely.

# If You Could Wish for Anything

Whenever darkness covered us completely, light always seemed to find a crack and stream through. One source of this light came under the heading of the Make-A-Wish Foundation, the generous organization renowned for its mission of making dreams come true for kids who suffer from life-threatening diseases. Lori knew of Make-A-Wish, and after John was diagnosed she contacted them.

When we moved to Westlake and were still driving John to his school in Santa Monica, we passed a business along the freeway that sold jungle gyms. John would pester us to check them out. He loved to climb and to explore. After he was diagnosed, when we asked him what he would want if he could have *anything*, it didn't take him long to say a jungle gym. Intuitively, at age nine, he chose something that would bring others to him. With its three swings, a rock-climbing wall, monkey bars, a slide, and a two-level fort with, embarrassingly, about the same square footage as our house, the jungle gym was quite a draw for his friends. While John stayed in his own backyard, his world expanded.

He wanted a sign that read "John and Ben's Hideout," but Make-A-Wish balked. The gift, after all, was for John, not for John and Ben. And Make-A-Wish didn't know that John lived not to possess, but to share. It was his wish to bring people into his life. The imaginative adventures that he shared with friends (and Ben) took him all around the world, spanning time and space. Continuously, he taught all of us this lesson: the real adventure of life is not to be found "out there", but within us, here and now. It is experienced with the five senses, but even more so with the heart. Faith, trust, and imagination allow life to transcend the material and fill it with meaning.

One of the gifts of the creative part of the brain is that it doesn't know what is real and what is not. For example, you go to a scary movie and your heart races, your palms sweat, you get nervous, and so on. (That's why I don't go to scary movies anymore. I work hard at not having those things happen.) The brain experiences the menace as real and sends all the correlating responses to the body.

So when John had adventures on the jungle gym with his friends, he experienced life fully. He saw himself as strong and capable, as embracing the struggle and finding victory. He was the hero of his own saga, but he did not ride away alone into the sunset. Rather, he brought his triumph home to his family. For John, no gain, no gift, could be claimed unless it was shared.

About two years later, in March 2002, Ben got his Make-A-Wish gift. Being a bit more outwardly adventurous, his first request was for a motorcycle. Still a boy, his need for speed (physically and emotionally) dominated his being. The Make-A-Wish representative came to our home and sat down with Ben at the kitchen table. She let him down gently.

Ben then asked for a car.

"Ben," she said, "no wheels."

"A boat?"

Finally, they found a compromise: a Disney cruise for the whole family.

The day before we left for Ben's Make-A-Wish cruise, a friend of Lori's invited the family to her home to be prayed over by a man she said had a powerful ministry. Carmelo Cortez was from a small village in the Philippines. As a young boy, he would travel to various houses and pray the Rosary with the sick, and eventually he began saving small donations to fulfill his heart's desire to build a church in his village.

The project took an intriguing turn after a wealthy woman gave him the land on which to build the church. When construction began, water came up from the ground. It smelled of roses and felt like oil. Greedily, the woman took the land back, but the oil ceased to come forth.

Then someone else donated land, and again, the oil came forth. Carmelo began taking rose petals, dipping them into the oil, and placing them on the chests of people who prayed for healing. Miraculously, various images appeared on the petals.

I believed in miracles. I had even begun to experience life itself as a miracle; love overcoming indifference or coldness as a miracle; joy in the midst of struggle as a miracle. Yet I also lived with the belief that God is sovereign. I never believed my prayers could control God's decisions, but I never doubted that physical healing was within the power of God; thus, we never turned down prayer. With all this in mind, we went to be prayed over by the devout Filipino.

We entered the ordinary house and found no incense, no organ music, no angels singing quietly in the background, only a bouquet of white roses on a table. After a few minutes, Carmelo entered.

"Take a rose," he said.

I selected one and gave it to him.

We began with a few simple prayers, the Our Father, a Hail Mary, but what occurred *was* miraculous. Unceremoniously, Carmelo dipped the rose petals into the oil and placed one on each of our chests. He anointed each of our foreheads and my hands with the oil. Then he left—walked

out of the room. He didn't levitate. He didn't even pro-
nounce a benediction in Latin, or any other language, for
that matter.

"Look at your petals," our host said when he returned.
We took them from our chests and found an impression
on each. On mine was an image of a mature-looking angel
holding his fist up (a protector or warrior); Lori's bore
Christ's face with a crown of thorns on His head; John's
showed an angelic angel with a boy's face (I recognize my
redundancy, but you have to have seen it); and Ben's held
a cute little angel, smaller than mine, but also with his fist
up (a little warrior).

No doubt, we all wanted to say something holy, or
at least profound, to commemorate what had just taken
place, but what came out was something like, "Wow!...
What does this mean?"

I'm not sure why my hands were anointed, but perhaps
it had to do with my music. I had been writing and recording for a while. Later that year, I completed a full-length
CD and began performing music rooted in my struggles
and in my faith.

In the car on the way home, we tried to make sense of
the experience. What did the miracle mean? Finally, John
said, "God just wants us to know that He's near and that
He's real."

Yup. That sounded right. Out of the mouths of babes ...

The next day, we took off for the cruise, as expected,
and it wasn't long before Ben was making waves on the
ship. When the captain posed for photographs with other
Make-A-Wish kids, all with various disabilities, Ben, who
could still see fairly well, paused, looked at the other kids,
and then refused to join the group for the picture.

"I'm not like them," he said.

Eventually they got him to pose, but at that point, his
Make-A-Wish was to be anywhere but where he was.

To this day, Ben struggles to accept his blindness and to recognize any disability in himself.

"Great!" some would say. "He's a fighter."

Others would say, "Poor child, he can't face reality."

I don't know what to say. At the time of this writing, Ben is twenty-two years old and almost completely blind. But he still asks his old man for a motorcycle, wants to take the family truck for a drive, and hopes to buy his own boat. His need for speed has not diminished in the least, but he knows when to slow down to offer support for those moving a bit slower.

At every opportunity, Ben extended his hand to lead John around—literally the blind leading the blind—and it sometimes ended with both of them walking into walls or falling down stairs. After a brief dusting off, they would laugh.

Ben still boasts of eating escargot on the Disney cruise ship, swimming in the Mickey pool beneath a star-swept sky, and playing furious games of ping-pong. (I think the ship lost quite a few balls over the rail during that week.) I believe Ben's fondest pleasures, however, were found nearer to home: playing roller hockey in the cul-de-sac, skateboarding at Papa Jack's Skatepark in Malibu, and frolicking in the cool waves at Zuma Beach.

The Disney cruise was a thrill for John, as well, but it wasn't the kind of experience that led to his greatest contentment. As John reminded us once we were home, no cruise could compare with the knowledge that God was near and cared.

# 12

# Boys' Night, a Birthday, and a Boat

One of our family traditions, started when the boys were very young, was Boys' Night. Now don't get me wrong. It wasn't that girls weren't allowed. They just didn't get to choose the menu or the movie. Cholesterol and body count were never considered when deciding on the food or the film. Lori often used the occasion to go out on her own, or with a friend, to see a movie or just to take a break. Boys' Night became a party night, on which the tears of the week would be balanced with laughter and a raucous good time. We made a conscious choice to find the small victories, the special days, which could be any day, and celebrate life. It wasn't hard, really. It just required making that choice.

To use a biblical allusion, Boys' Night consisted of killing the fatted calf (buying some beef, really) and burning it to smithereens on the barbecue. The festival included loud music, wrestling matches (and sometimes falling over chairs), dancing (and sometimes falling over chairs), burp contests (completing whole sentences with a single burp usually got the prize), and sodas (necessary fuel for the burp contests). This part of the evening was usually followed by a very male movie, usually involving gladiators, aliens, or man-eating dinosaurs. No real surprise that Lori chose to miss these nights.

Birthdays were also cause for major celebrations in the Sikorra household. In fact, I've been known to plan my own surprise parties, usually a few months before the day. At one such party, however, I was outmaneuvered by my family. Even I couldn't have planned a surprise so grand.

"Come out to the street, Joe," Lori said. She was trying to suppress a smile but was failing. She looked giddy.

I was confused. I hadn't planned any surprises for myself on the street. Slowly, all our guests made their way outside. I brought up the rear, and as I stepped out the door, I saw a beautiful eighteen-foot Sea Ray boat. Attached to the boat dealer's pickup truck, it had been backed down our little street until the magic moment. The boys started shrieking (or maybe that was me). I helped John and Ben climb inside, and then we all got in. I couldn't stop rubbing my hands all over it. I may have even made my wife jealous.

My friends Clint and Carla had given me a boat. A boat! Eighteen feet of beauty.

"How could this be?" I kept asking no one in particular. I really couldn't comprehend such generosity.

Clint kept telling me that it was a gift he hoped would bring my family some joy and happiness as we struggled with the boys' illness. I was deeply humbled. Later, we pushed the boat into the garage. (Well, the others pushed. I refused to get out from behind the driver's seat.) It just barely fit. I sat in the boat late into the night, long after our friends left. I imagined the adventures yet to come—lakes, rivers, waterskiing. Mostly, I thought about the selflessness of Clint and Carla's act.

Our friends had not given out of financial abundance, for they had none, but from hearts overflowing with compassion, love, and generosity. They understood our desire to give the boys every opportunity to experience life's fullness and beauty. They understood that it was in the life-giving water where we as a family played the most and found healing. They wanted to give us the chance to create powerful, lasting memories.

Their generosity reminded me of the woman Jesus pointed out to His disciples. She gave the equivalent of a couple of pennies as an offering at the temple. But Jesus said, "Truly, I say to you, this poor widow has put in more than all those who are contributing to the treasury. For they all contributed out of their abundance; but she out of her poverty has put in everything she had, her whole living" (Mk 12:43–44). On any level, the boat was an extremely generous gift. But it was especially so because it was prompted by love.

We took the boat to many California lakes tucked away in the majestic Sierra Nevada, the mountain range stretching northward from the Mojave Desert to the Cascades. We explored Lake Mohave, surrounded by desert terrain and fed by the mighty Colorado River. We took our little boat into the deep blue Pacific Ocean to the Channel Islands, some eleven miles off the California coast, whose marine life ranges from microscopic plankton to the blue whale, the largest animal on earth.

Even as the boys became blind, their enthusiasm never waned when it came to boating. They would sit in the open bow with their faces turned toward the warmth of the sun. They beamed and laughed as we plowed through and over waves; they shouted with glee when spray kicked up from wind and waves showered them. When it was calmer, they would hang their heads over the sides and listen to the boat cutting through the water. They seemed to be as transfixed and transported by the experience as I was.

How can anyone witness the beauty of nature and think of the earth as just a cosmic accident? It is design incarnate.

One might reasonably ask what good is natural beauty to boys who cannot see it. My answer is that sharing those boating excursions, with whatever senses were available to experience them, brought us closer as a family. And I, who could see the resplendent creation all around us, including the delight of my sons, was reminded of the One who made it all, which inspired awe, gratitude, and trust.

During our boating adventures, God's magnificent creation, from the smallest microorganism to the largest star, spoke to my heart. Natural beauty penetrated my soul and gave me a glimpse of who God is, because His creatures speak of Him, of His care for them. Gradually I came to understand that if the smallest of His living creatures, such as plankton, fit into His plan, then so must I. My orientation began to shift from feeling as if I was the one who needed to do all the caring to feeling myself cared for. I began to believe that I was part of something magnificent. And the more I felt loved by God, the more freely I loved.

Up to this point, I had focused on the sacrifices I needed to make to care for my boys and my wife. And I felt as if I had been beaten down by the blows that had come my way, because in focusing on myself I had forgotten how God had sacrificed Himself to bring me into His family; how He had taken the really big hits so that I could live in freedom; and how He continuously provided for us. As my encounters with nature reminded me of these truths, I began to shift my attitude. I wasn't resigning myself to the doom determined by some capricious, impersonal fate; I was entering into a grand, perfect plan, designed for my happiness by the ultimate Designer, who loved me. Embracing my role in caring for my family was important, but feeling cared for and cherished by a loving God moved me from mere resignation to joyful acceptance of His will for me.

I would like to say this insight hit me like a ton of bricks and stayed with me, but that wasn't the case. My confidence in divine providence grew slowly and with difficulty. First, I had to give up my idea of who I was. I had to begin to see myself, my family, and my purpose with a vision beyond what my eyes could see or what my mind could imagine, and to accept that there was a higher view with perfect perspective: God's view. Contemplating the complexity and splendor of creation helped me to appreciate that God's view is vaster than mine. Next, I began to pray for glimpses of this higher vision, wherein I could see His love for me and my role in His creation. I wasn't always successful. In fact, I was barely successful. Perhaps I wasn't ready to be loved so deeply. But my appetite for greater faith had been whetted, fueled.

We were able to use the boat for ten years, but then we had to sacrifice it to buy a much-needed van. Our transportation needs had changed. Our sons' needs had changed. But the boat was the gift that kept giving. It took us, me, beyond any shoreline. It connected me with eternity and still does so.

# 13

# A Seed Is Buried

I was watching my dog bury a bone—or maybe it was my running shoe again; I don't know—and it got me thinking about some words of Jesus in the Gospel of John: "Truly, truly, I say to you, unless a grain of wheat falls into the earth and dies, it remains alone; but if it dies, it bears much fruit. He who loves his life loses it, and he who hates his life in this world will keep it for eternal life" (12:24–25).

Despite my growing belief that I was part of a larger plan, I still held on to anger, disappointment, and sadness, among other things. I was still clinging to life selfishly, so that I wasn't able to be as reckless in my love as I knew I should be. Sooner or later, my refusal to let go completely would destroy me.

Not that all my "selfish" desires were bad. I desired health for my boys, for example. Yet despite my desire and my prayers, the disease had them both in its grip. John was almost completely blind, and Ben was only a few steps behind him. Neither of them worked anywhere near their grade level in school. How could I hold on to the desire that they be well and not cause myself—and them—frustration and disappointment?

It was difficult to remember that God's ways are frequently different from mine. My ways seemed to be the ones that would achieve good results for now, but God has eternity in mind. To avoid harming myself and my boys, I needed to accept God's way of seeing things and doing things and to let go of my own. I needed to trust in His wisdom and to appreciate the gifts that He chose to send us, including Batten disease. "Unless a grain of wheat . . ." The seed must die. The seed—our lives, our desires—*must* die so that we can be reborn into eternal life.

My heart was being spoken to, challenged. *Embrace the struggle, Joe. Let the tears live alongside the joy. Let go. Be reckless in your love. The seed must be buried, or it will remain just a seed.*

One way God helped me to understand the need to give up my life in order to find it was through my seeing the process at work in my sons. John's and Ben's abilities and bodies were in continual decline. But I came to believe that God was bringing forth beauty, growth, and abundance, for I saw it in fleeting glimpses. I saw that as my boys were dying in some ways, their potential to transform others, including me, was growing.

Many people around us seemed touched and moved by the presence of our boys. They gave others the opportunity to be patient, kind, and generous. We attended church each week and usually attracted more attention than we really wanted. Guiding blind children to Communion usually got people looking. But the boys would smile when people grabbed them to whisper a hello. Ben would sometimes hold up the song sheets while doing his own version of what was being sung. "They're such beautiful boys," we would often hear.

Our sons brought out the better side of Lori and me too. Yet I simultaneously felt myself sinking, as if being pushed down by a terrible weight of sadness. I'm not sure whether anyone saw it, but my soul was being crushed. I was doing my best to love, but I didn't feel love, God's love. I *knew* it was there, but I didn't *feel* it. There is no getting around the fact that dying feels like, well, dying. In the midst of my desolation, however, my heart was being spoken to, challenged: *Embrace the struggle, Joe. Let the tears live alongside the joy. Let go. Be reckless in your love. The seed must be buried, or it will remain just a seed.*

In November 1999, our dear friend Bob Maurer sponsored a weekend trip to SeaWorld in San Diego. Although John had lost most of his sight, and wasn't able to see even the giant killer whales, he could feel the splashes, hear the sounds, and catch the excitement of the crowd. And his enthusiasm equaled, or even surpassed, that of those who could see.

I have a photograph of the boys standing before the glass separating them from a huge orca. Ben is squatting as he peers into the tank—he could still see enough to be impressed by the sights—and the whale is passing by just a few feet away from him. John is standing next to his brother, completely absorbed. I'm not sure how, but he was taking it all in.

Some of the people around us noticed John with an expression of wonder on their faces. While viewing the whales, the onlookers were struck by the natural beauty of the animals—their size, speed, and strength. Looking at John, were they perhaps moved by supernatural beauty—the divine life that filled his soul?

John jumped at the offer to get into a pool with the dolphins. Ben, on the other hand, didn't trust the dolphins enough to share a bath with them. For all of Ben's love of adventure, his plastic four-inch shark in a tub full of suds, doing battle with the dinosaur of the same size, was all the swimming with critters he wanted. His ability to see the dolphins made him fear them, which held him back from an amazing experience. John's blindness, on the other hand, gave him radical trust. How did seeing, and fearing, hold me back, I wondered.

Dressed in wet suits provided by Sea World, John and I got into the pool. John allowed his hand to be placed on the dolphins that were led to him. He was captivated by them as he touched their smooth bodies and felt their breath. People watched him and smiled. Some, I heard, had tears in their eyes. John became more of an attraction than the dolphins.

Lori, wanting to give her sons more than just enough, asked a trainer after the whale show if the boys could feel the whale. A crazy request. Reckless love. And it was rewarded. When the giant orca opened its mouth, John felt its tongue. (I'm glad his hand didn't smell like a tuna sandwich or a seal.) Again, John exhibited no fear. Ben, on the other hand, chose not to get so intimate.

Lori didn't stop there. After every show, she would boldly approach anyone she saw as having authority and explain our situation. Moved by the story, the person would lead us backstage. The boys weren't denied anything. They seemed to bring out the best in people.

There were those who recoiled, however. Did their seeing the boys' condition arouse feelings of awkwardness, repulsion, even fear? As normal as these reactions are, they were painful for us to bear.

Even harder to accept were these reactions from people close to us. As the boys' illness progressed, some people distanced themselves from us because they could no longer bear the intensity that came with being our friends. Others moved out of our lives when the boys could no longer continue with certain activities. Either way, these losses hurt, as did the recognition that the common ground needed to sustain friendships was giving way beneath our boys' feet slowly but continually.

Lori and I understood—it was sad, not only for others but also for us, to see other young lives blossom and
branch out as our boys seemed to wither. But were they
only withering? As one form of life was dying, was not
another being born?

The path my boys were given is rare and difficult, and
to walk alongside them required a deliberate choice. But
those who stuck around were richly rewarded, because the
seed that dies bears much fruit that feeds many.

# 14

# Going into the Deep

Even though Lori and I never pushed our boys (at least not too much), they clamored for adventure. In the summer of 2002, John heard that his best childhood friends were joining the Junior Lifeguard Program.

"Can I, Mom and Dad?"

Saint John, wanting to save souls and bad swimmers.

"Well, remember, you'd be a *junior* guard. I think that's when you learn to save yourself."

"Oh, okay."

John had already lost about 95 percent of his sight. He could distinguish bright light from darkness and see some things as shadowed objects, but that's about it. Nevertheless, he was allowed to try out for the Junior Lifeguard Program. He was required to swim one hundred yards, then ten more underwater, then tread water for five minutes.

As John had about 4 percent body fat, he was given a concession: to wear a wet suit. (I think the lifeguards secretly wanted him to wear it for floatation, in case he had a seizure in the water. If he sank, the headlines would not be pretty.)

John passed the tryout and then dove into the training. It was a foggy summer, and the water was cold, but he met each day with a smile. He fought his way through the surf into the deep blue, guided toward a buoy by a strong, encouraging voice on the beach.

"Swim left, John! Keep going! A little right! No! The other right!"

The professional guards were nearby in case John lost his way completely, but he performed admirably. Alongside seventy-five other kids, he raced up and down the beach (while holding hands with an assistant or a buddy), learned about the ocean and its inhabitants, and pitted his eighty pounds of pure muscle against the crushing waves. He never talked about how he was different from the other kids, in that he couldn't see. He just did what was asked of him.

John did well not only because he was physically strong, but also because he was willing to persevere, believed in the value of what he was doing, and knew that he was loved. He trusted in the love of those who cared for him and in the love of God.

Are we any different from John? We too can do amazing things with the gifts God gives us. But if we can't hear His voice or sense His protection, we fear our limitations when we face challenges out in the deep.

When Saint Peter saw Jesus walking on the water, he knew it was a miraculous feat, impossible without the power of God. Yet, despite the fierce wind and waves, Peter, in what almost seems like a challenge to Jesus, said, "Lord, if it is you, bid me come to you on the water" (Mt 14:28). Peter couldn't psyche himself up to walk on water. He couldn't figure out the best water-walking technique. Only by listening to God could he do the impossible.

"Come," Jesus said.

And Peter got out of the boat and walked on the water—that is, until he took his eyes off Jesus and looked down at the waves. In mere moments Peter went from

doing the impossible to doing the probable—sinking in
fear. Jesus pulled him to safety and said, "O you of little
faith, why did you doubt?" (Mt 14:31).

Jesus is saying the same thing to us today: "Act not on
what you think you can do but on what I can do for you.
Keep your focus on me, and trust."

John didn't look at the powerful waves, at the buoy
in the distance. He simply trusted, listened, and obeyed.
Did it help that he couldn't see? If you were about to
swim in the ocean blindfolded, would the courage you
need come from your lack of sight? Or would it come
from the professional lifeguards telling you, "You can
do this, and if you sink, we'll be there for you." Perhaps
blindness gave John the opportunity to trust, but the fact
is, he chose to trust.

John enjoyed Junior Lifeguards for several summers. He
even won awards in the Junior Lifeguards Ironman con-
test, which included competing in five training events in
one day. And Lori and I didn't really mind the hours we
*had* to spend on the beach, either.

In continuing to be active and in following his passions,
John set the bar high for all of us. He became the family
standard-bearer for listening to that voice that says, "Step
out of the boat, and keep your eyes on me. If you listen to
your fears and start to sink, I will pull you up. Trust me."

# 15

# Letting Go

We knew that wheelchairs would eventually be a part of our lives. Thus, we realized we would need to find a house with bedrooms downstairs—or at least enough space downstairs for the family to sleep. By the grace of God, we sold our house quickly and bought another one a few miles away. We originally called the "new" house the Battleship Sikorra, as it was somewhat dilapidated and painted an inglorious gray. The carpets crumbled when we walked on them. But the house had "a lot of potential". (That's real-estate talk for a fixer-upper.)

After the move, John began second grade at the local public school a couple of blocks away, and Ben seized command of the local kindergarten. We tried to hold our heads high while our hearts sank, for John's former Catholic school was three blocks in the opposite direction from his new school. Thankfully, we quickly established some deep friendships with families who shared our faith. And another huge blessing entered our life at this time, and remained throughout the boys' school years. Her name was Linda Jacobson.

Linda was the vision specialist with the school district. Since Ben wasn't showing signs of deteriorating eyesight at this time, she met with him only to make his acquaintance. Eventually she met with both boys weekly. She would take them separately to a vacant classroom and teach them braille. The boys didn't take to it, and we didn't push them to try harder. Given their prognosis, they would never become great readers. We simply wanted them to be mentally challenged and engaged for as long as possible.

Occasionally Linda gave the boys nifty tools, such as talking calculators and special tape players with recordings of books, to use in school and at home. When she gave them mobility canes for the blind, they thought they were the best light sabers ever. Later, when they learned that the canes were to help them navigate, they shunned them completely. They would pack them in their backpacks, where they would remain. For them the cane was an outward sign of a struggle they preferred to keep private.

When the boys had meltdowns at school, Linda was the first to respond. She wiped away their tears of frustration and cheered and praised their every success. She did the same for the boys' teachers and for Lori and me too. None of us had experienced blind children before.

Amazingly, Linda had taught two other boys (also brothers) with Batten disease. The chances of this happening are about one in a billion. Most of the doctors we knew had never even heard of the disease. Linda's presence in our lives served as further evidence that we had been led to Westlake Village by divine providence. Lori and I could never fully express our gratitude for her.

Linda not only met our needs but anticipated them, as we walked somewhat aimlessly and blindly—all four of us—though the public education system. When we didn't know that the boys needed mobility specialists or machines to enlarge print or any number of things, Linda did. And she would step in at just the right moment, make the right things happen, and then fade into the background. She was a rock, and she fought for her kids, our kids, while assuring us that all would be well. "They will be all right. You will be all right," she would say with a smile, sounding a bit like Teresa of Avila.

But Saint Teresa also said that, when we get to heaven, life on earth will seem like merely one bad night in a lousy hotel. In other words, yes, ultimately we all will be all right, but in the meantime we might have to endure fleas in the bed.

John's vision deteriorated so much that he was unable to walk to or from school by himself. "My eyes don't work so good," he would tell his friends, "but my ears are really great." Little by little, his mind also diminished. Batten disease causes a progressive death of cells, especially in the brain. And as these cells die, so does the ability to learn, to process information, to reason.

Although John was a likable kid, he had a hard time keeping friendships. Boys naturally want to go out and do things, to explore the world. John shared this desire but was quickly losing the ability to act on it. And rare was the boy who would hold himself back in order to play with John or to offer his arm and say, "Come on, John. I'll lead you." Some truly extraordinary kids entered John's life and loved him dearly, but understandably his disease exacted a high price even from these remarkable relationships.

As mentioned previously, Lori and I lost friends too, as friendships among adults raising children often spring from their kids' sporting events or school activities or public achievements. The narrowing of our social circle was hard on me, a born extrovert. Lori would say that I was naturally joyful and that our burdens and losses were easier for me to bear than for her. But, in fact, I was struggling as much as anyone else in the family.

Sometimes when we felt especially hurt or disappointed, I would make everyone a glass of Miracle Milk (warm milk and honey). With moonlight cascading through the kitchen window, and the boys dressed in their jammies, we would speak of heaven—the place of perfect love and eternal joy with God and each other.

During one such Miracle Milk conversation, John said, "I don't want to go to heaven. God won't let me take my body, and I won't be able to play."

"Play?" I said. "Oh, John, the things we'll be able to do will make Luke Skywalker and Superman look like wimps. We'll get new bodies that never wear out and eyes that can see from here to eternity."

Little by little, we were learning to let go of this world and to place our hopes in the one to come.

*Ben (2) and John (5), Pacific Palisades, California, 1996*

*Ben giving John an unwanted lecture on the way to Lourdes, France, 2003*

*John sporting his new pair of glasses on the day he began first grade, 1998*

*Ben and John at Sea World in San Diego, California, 1999*

*Ben (6) up to bat*

*Ben and John with Bessie, who sometimes brought the smiles*
*when nothing else could*

*Joe and John water skiing when John's physical abilities began to diminish but not his lust for adventure, Fontana Lake, North Carolina, 2008*

*Ben wake-boarding on Fontana Lake, North Carolina, 2008*

*John skiing with the help of Joe and some spectacular men and women who help the disabled to stay active, 2008*

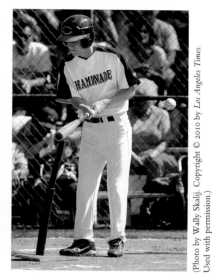

*John, Chaminade High School Homecoming King, 2010*

*John at bat on May 13, 2010*

*John and Joe, hand in hand, taking home on May 13, 2010*

*John and Joe on the field at Dodger Stadium, 2010*

*John, mostly confined to a wheelchair but still smiling, with Lori, 2015*

*Although too blind to play football, Ben in his Agoura High School team uniform with John and their friend Alison Kale, 2008*

*From the sidelines, Ben rooting for his classmates at Agoura High School*

*Caregiver Bobby Moin and Ben at California Lutheran, which let Ben take classes, full scholarship, and help their football team, 2016*

*Last family photograph with both boys, Malibu, California, 2014*

# 16

# To Share the Cross

As a police officer I frequently became involved in the lives of people who were suffering as much as, if not more than, I was. With its mild climate, Santa Monica has quite a number of homeless, and since many of them have psychiatric problems, answering an emergency call involving a homeless person usually meant dealing with mental illness.

On a typical warm, sunny Santa Monica day, a homeless man, with shaved head and tattooed body, threatened to jump from the bluffs facing the ocean down to the Pacific Coast Highway a couple of hundred feet below. Along the cliff was a park, which was separated from the precipice by a fence, and the suicidal man was on the dangerous side of the fence. This call was high priority not only because the man could kill himself but also because he could seriously injure others, by landing on a car, for example.

I arrived at the park with a bunch of officers, while other officers stopped the highway traffic below. We knew that a good resolution to the situation could not be rushed, even though the California Highway Patrol was upset about the freeway backing up. Oh, well. They would just need to tell the sure-to-be-impatient drivers, "Welcome to Los Angeles."

At the park spectators began to gather. Why go to the movies when you can watch the outlandish in person?

The officers took up various positions along the fence while maintaining some cover. The jumper, after all, had armed himself with a knife, sharpened glass, and a bottle of cheap wine. Some officers were assigned to use lethal force should circumstances dictate, and others were armed with Tasers or other nonlethal weapons.

In a piercing voice, the man threatened, "I'll jump! Stay back!"

And the hostage negotiators (although only the traffic was being held hostage) said smart things such as "Don't jump" and "Really. We mean it. Don't do it."

Meanwhile, as the minutes rolled on and the highway traffic built up, I thought equally smart things such as "I wonder if I'll make it home for dinner" and "I guess I didn't really need to eat lunch."

But, seriously, my higher self recognized the sanctity and the value of life—of this person's life. Behind the ranting and the tattoos was a man in serious pain. Silently, I began to pray.

Someone of very high rank came up with an idea: "I bet he's hungry. Let's bribe him with McDonald's, get him close to the fence, then grab him."

The prescribed Quarter Pounder was purchased, and we all had a good laugh when the jumper raced in, grabbed his meal, and moved away before anyone could get close to him. This guy was the *real* Hamburglar. Well, at least someone got to eat.

After he finished his burger, the jumper pointed at me and said, "I want to talk to a Christian cop! I want to talk to him!"

I looked around. There was only one "him" in the immediate vicinity. And he was *me*.

Why me? I had a gun pointed at his head. But clearly, he was looking beyond the gun, beyond the uniform.

As the jumper walked toward me, I probably said something profound such as "Uh . . . how about we take you to a padded cell and lock you away for years?"

No. Not really. I can't remember what I said. But we talked.

The other cops were amused that the jumper wanted to talk to the "Christian cop". I had never spoken to this man before, he did not know who I was, but the Lord works in mysterious ways.

After a while, the man got bored with the conversation and began to rant in his loudest voice. But my partners and I were able to coax him to an area where we could sneak up from behind and tackle him safely to the ground.

As the normal flow of cars resumed on the highway, and the crowds slowly dispersed to get on with their normal lives, I took the man to the hospital, where I would put a psych hold on him and he would continue to wrestle with his tortured existence. On the way, we talked about schizophrenia, demonic possession, the Dodgers, and tattoos. Both of us had returned to our normal lives too.

Another time, I was sent to an alley where a drunken transient was reportedly unable to care for himself. His condition was deplorable—crippled by neuropathy, drunk beyond description, and covered in days, perhaps weeks, of filth and his own excrement. Yet still, there was goodness in the man. How did I see it? Not through my eyes alone, I assure you. God gave me the sight to see what I could not see by myself.

If I had simply called the paramedics and left, the man would have been given emergency care and released. I decided to take a different route. After the paramedics checked him out, I somehow got him into my car and drove him to a hospital a couple of cities away, a psych hospital where he could get longer-term help. During the drive, he agreed to be admitted as a danger to himself. (No doubt, this statement was true.) When we arrived, though, the psych ward wouldn't admit him until he had sobered up a little. Well, a lot. The amount of alcohol in his system—more than five times the legal limit to drive a car—would kill most people.

Nevertheless, we spoke of God, faith, and family. He was a believer who had lost faith in himself. He allowed me to reach out to his family back East, but he refused to be seen by them in his condition. Unfortunately, his condition never improved. When he was able to leave the hospital, a day or two after being admitted, he returned to the streets, to live in alleys and under boxes as a slave to cheap booze.

I saw Herbye (we were on a first-name basis) a few times after our original meeting, and each time he talked about making a change. But he did not have the strength to stop drinking, and he was not willing to accept help from anyone. During one of our frank discussions, he said that he blamed no one but himself for the state he was in. His bad decisions had turned him into an alcoholic. But I believed in the mercy of God, that God could help Herbye, if Herbye would only let Him.

Herbye died within the year, yards from the hospital. His mother and sisters called me and asked if I would come to his memorial. They wanted to scatter his ashes over the Pacific Ocean, which Herbye loved. The police department was kind enough to let me go on duty, in uniform.

As the boat slowly made its way out of the harbor, we passed impressive mansions along the coastline. It's amazing how squalor and abundance can live in such close proximity. It's also amazing how faith and doubt, and despair and hope can reside next to each other too. Years later, when I spoke with Herbye's mother, Rose, then ninety-two, she still mourned the loss of her son, but she knew with certainty that we would all be reunited one day in a better place. And her hope, born of faith in a merciful God and probably countless prayers for her son, brought her much comfort.

As a police officer, I had many other encounters with brokenness, struggle, and death, and ironically, in spite of the stress and the exhaustion they caused, they sometimes helped me to carry my own burdens. I often felt alone in my suffering. After all, how many families have two children with incurable, degenerative diseases? But being able to connect with and help others who suffered offered me a sense of purpose beyond that of caring for my own family and cemented my belief that I really was here on earth to serve God.

What, I sometimes asked myself, is the difference between those who rise above their difficulties and those, like Herbye, who remain stuck? You can point to good breaks and bad fortune, but is there more to our lives than luck? It seemed to me that those who overcome adversity are those who accept help from beyond themselves. So another takeaway from police work was the realization that if my family was going survive our challenges, we would need to accept support from others, no matter how humbling that might be. We would need to let God, and His people, lift us up. Our job was to cooperate, to see the possibilities. Others before us had gone down tough roads. Our job was to learn from them.

My cop job brought me joy in the most surprising ways. It put me in contact not only with people who needed my help, but also with co-workers who had committed their lives to service. Loneliness, despair, and depression are friends of isolation. Hope, joy, and love are found in connection: connection with God, connection with His people.

## 17

# When Light Fades

One Saturday morning when John was ten, Lori and I were lying in bed. John crawled in beside us (Ben was probably outside trying to figure out how to climb onto the roof) and began talking about colors and images, all of which were fading for him. "What does a baseball field look like?"

Our bedroom window faced a baseball field, and the sounds of youthful players hitting balls and excited parents cheering them wafted into our room. John wanted to retain what his brain knew was going on out there.

"What color are my eyes, Mommy?"

"You have beautiful green eyes like me," Lori said.

"What do yours look like?"

"Look closely."

With his face inches from hers, he said, "Your face looks red. I can't really see it." He ran his hands softly through her long brown hair. "What color is your hair?"

Silently, Lori began to cry.

At times John had a peace about him that transcended human understanding. Once, when he was feeling sad about his lack of sight, and my heart was breaking for him, I said, "John, if I could give you my eyes, I would."

"Oh no, Daddy. I would never let you do that. It's too bad."

Silence hung in the air. How was I to respond to that? All that pain, yet he would rather keep it than inflict it on another. I would like to take the credit for teaching him this kind of love. But I cannot. This kind of perfect love can come only from God.

At other times, John lamented his losses bitterly. One day we heard a loud knock at the door. It was a burly sheriff's deputy.

"We got a call from this location. A young boy."

Normally I would automatically call out, "Ben! Did you call the police? (Again?)" But Ben was outside, maybe trying to set free the goldfish in the community pool. John walked into the room. He was scared.

"I'm mad that no one is trying to fix my eyes," he said.

You couldn't argue with him. He felt desperate.

While the boys' vision tapered quickly, their enthusiasm, for the most part, did not.

"Tell me," John would ask, "what do you see?"

Rather than lie and say, "Oh, not much," we would describe sights as best we could. We didn't want him to feel as if he were missing out. But he was. We would have magnified the loss, however, if we had held back.

In Yosemite, for example, where we traveled for many years, I would describe the wildlife along these lines: "John, about a hundred yards away there is a coyote. His hair is long, his tail is bushy, and he's standing on a rock."

Later, when recounting the adventure, he would say with great enthusiasm, "Remember when *we* saw that coyote, and he was ..."

He "saw" through our eyes. Our sons experienced what we experienced because we shared all that we could with them. And, to be honest, it drained us completely.

When people give and give until they can't give anymore, they tend to bury their feelings. They must, because they simply do not have enough energy to deal with them. But those emotions are still there, and they can turn up in some interesting places.

Lori dealt with her emotions in the garden. She worked up a sweat by digging, weeding, and planting—transforming neglected and unwanted shrubbery into beautiful flower beds. She dug furiously at times, and then she planted with tender, loving care. A few days later she would dig up what she had planted and put it somewhere else.

In the garden Lori could bring order out of chaos. There she found a dominion that she could control somewhat. And the work needed to keep plants alive and fruitful, such as weeding and pruning, became metaphors for the painful but necessary processes going on in her life.

I mowed the lawn, which was symbolic of, well, to be honest, nothing. The grass simply needed to be cut once a week. Years later, Lori fired me as the lawn man. Perhaps she wanted me to share more in her process, but we each needed to find our own way to work through our feelings.

And so, as I mentioned earlier, I wrote music—sad songs, songs of gratitude, songs of questioning, and songs for my boys. When I scraped together enough money, I would record them in a studio.

"Winter" was one of the first songs I recorded. "It's winter and cold. Feeling weary, weak, and old. Though I've eyes yet to see, can't see what I'm to be." No mystery to those lyrics. Years later my songs took on a more spring and summer theme. "Take time, find little ways. Feel the Son, enjoy the days." I was growing. I was experiencing more hope and joy, though my circumstances were still overwhelming at times.

Initially, I wrote music as my own personal reflection on and exploration of my faith. Later I discovered, while in concert or when asked to sing one of my songs at a funeral or another event, that my music was meant to be shared. Our faith and our talents are meant not only for ourselves but also for the building up of others in the community.

Having a creative outlet for my feelings, I was taken by surprise when raw emotions came to the surface from time to time. One day, when Ben was about seven, he was cautiously riding his scooter up and down the street. He had enough vision to navigate without running into too many things—usually—but on this day he bumped into something expensive.

We were having a birthday celebration with a few friends when Ben came into the house a little upset. I was probably trying to put out the fire in the barbecue, so my friend Dave, a great guy and a fellow police officer, discovered that Ben had run into a car, causing a little damage. The only problem was that the car was a Porsche and the owner flipped out.

Dave talked to the man and calmed him down, but when I found out that he had yelled at Ben and made him feel bad, I spent a few seconds doing some emotional knuckle crunching before heading down to the guy's house, where I intended to knock his head off his shoulders. But Dave ran interference again. Smiling and placing a hand on my shoulder, he said, "It's not worth it. It's okay."

The amount of anger I was experiencing was something new for me. I have a long fuse, and I am not given to emotional outbursts. So when I wanted to punish a man who had a good reason to be upset, I realized he wasn't really the source of my anger. He just gave me an opportunity to vent it. Luckily, that opportunity was thwarted.

Many of us have no doubt been carried away by strong emotions without understanding their true source and figuring out the appropriate response to the situation. But whenever we allow ourselves to act on emotions without thinking first, we risk sabotaging our relationships and undermining our happiness.

Here is a classic example of the destructive power of emotions in a marriage. A wife complains to her preoccupied husband that he never talks to her anymore. He responds to her criticism by communicating with her even less than he did before. She protests more, and he moves further away. The spouses are not aware that they are reacting to unresolved feelings, such as sadness, fear, or anger, lurking beneath the surface. Rather than talking honestly to each other about their feelings, and the things in their lives that might be causing them, they are turning each other into the enemy to be attacked or avoided.

Even when the underlying causes of our emotions are acknowledged, our feelings need to be brought under our control so that they do not control us. Gandhi said, "It is not that I do not get angry. I don't give vent to my anger. I cultivate the quality of patience as angerlessness, and generally speaking, I succeed. But I only control my anger when it comes. How I find it possible to control it would be a useless question, for it is a habit that everyone must cultivate and must succeed in forming by constant practice."[1]

Anger is powerful and potentially dangerous. No wonder Christian tradition names it one of the seven *deadly* sins, which each of us must learn to overcome. Since I'm not Gandhi, I can't conquer my weaknesses on my own. I need God to help me, and He does so in various ways. My anger at the Porsche owner was so intense that I was about to slug the guy, and thankfully, in my moment of need, a friend came to my rescue.

---

[1] Mohandas K. Gandhi, *All Men Are Brothers* (London: Bloomsbury Academic, 2005), 105.

# 18

# Angels among Us

John transitioned into middle school. Instead of walking a couple of blocks to school, he now had to be driven a couple of miles. Not far, but everything seemed to be moving away from us as the boys continued to diminish. Yet, as they lost their abilities, along with some of their friends, they gained other companions.

One afternoon I took John to the home of our new friends the Henzgens. I had met Tom Henzgen about ten years earlier, when we attended the Reserve Police Academy. Tom went on to become a paramedic and a firefighter, and we lost touch, but providentially we met again at church one Sunday.

Tom and I were in the garage working on some project, while TJ, Tom's son, and John played inside the house. The garage was full of workbenches, saws, hydraulic tools to lift, and other tools to grind and crunch. We did our best to fill the air with as many mechanical sounds as possible. Tom was handling a power something-or-other, and I stood alongside him, acting as if I knew what I was doing.

Over the cacophony of noise, we heard a loud "Dad!" We ran inside and found TJ holding John, whose body was convulsing violently and uncontrollably. A grand mal seizure is scary to watch, particularly when your son is the person having one. I took John into my arms and

held him until his body stopped shaking. Left unconscious, he sucked in huge gulps of air as his body tried
to recover from the physical assault that had emanated
from deep inside and had deprived him of oxygen. Sweat
formed on his face. A vicious blow to a little body. John
was thirteen.

As this was his first seizure (with many yet to come), we
called 911. We had been told this day would arrive, but
my foreknowledge had not prepared me for the shock *I*
would experience. The seizure came like a bolt out of the
blue, and it made me feel frightened and helpless. After it
was over, I sat quietly, with tears running down my face as
John struggled, it seemed to me, just to breathe.

We had entered another phase of Batten disease.

In the ambulance, I called Lori. The timing could not
have been worse for her: she was at an orientation in the
intensive care unit at the hospital. She was returning to
nursing, to one of the most demanding positions out there.
Surrounded by staff she didn't know, she walked out of the
unit and never returned. Her personal life was demanding
enough; a rigorous professional life would have to take
a backseat.

TJ could have ended the friendship after that. He had
seen John at one of his most frightening moments, and
more were on the way. Yet TJ didn't call it quits. He
embraced John and remained a steadfast friend. And he
wasn't the only one. Chrissy, TJ's sister (and John's prom
and homecoming date for several years), Paul, Andy, and
Alison stayed close despite the seizures and the other symptoms of Batten disease.

John began having seizures every seven to ten days, and
often at inopportune times: while riding a bike, running
on a track, swimming, and eating. We, and those around
the boys, had to become vigilant. Luckily, we were not

alone. God provided us with companions because, as John reminded us, God wants us to know that He's around and that He cares.

The following summer, Lori took the boys to Santa Monica Beach. Friends had come to town and decided it was a great time to do some bike riding at the beach. It was a perfect day. The sun warmed the body, and the beauty warmed the soul. The beach was sprawling and could easily accommodate the masses who thronged to the ocean. The towering waves rolled up on shore, providing all the fun a swimmer or surfer could want. It looked like a scene out of a movie. Oh, that's right, it *was* a place where movies were made.

John rode on the back of a tandem bike with our friend Chris. They were zipping up the path, no doubt fueled by John's calls of "Faster, faster!" Lori was about a hundred yards behind them. Between her and them, her girlfriend Jodie had Ben on another tandem.

Up ahead, Lori saw a commotion. She suspected—she knew—it involved John. He had been unlike his usual self all morning. As if by a giant wave crashing on the shore and then receding back into the ocean, Lori's temporary tranquility was washed away. As a nurse, Lori was no stranger to medical trauma, but it was different when it involved her own child. As she peddled faster, she prayed, "Please, God, give me peace, give me calm. I have to be able to think clearly."

By the time Lori reached John, a crowd had gathered. John was on the ground, seizing and tangled in the bike. Lori asked a stranger, who just happened to be an EMT, "Did you see how he fell? Should I call the paramedics?"

"I would," he said. "He came off the bike pretty hard and landed on the back of his neck." Of course, both boys (and adults) wore helmets.

As Lori fought for calm, she tried to comfort and care for John.

"Oh please, God ..."

A man reached over Lori's shoulder, placed his hand on John's head, and prayed quietly. Then he whispered into Lori's ear, "This is an angel."

Immediately, Lori was flooded with peace and calm. She looked up into the man's face and *knew* that he was John's angel. He had olive skin, dark curly hair, beautiful European features, and a brand-new blue Dodgers cap on his head. (Given his description, Lori probably wished he were her angel too.) The man took off his bright lime-green jacket and laid it over John. Then he moved about fifty feet away and sat cross-legged on the beach.

As the paramedics loaded John into the ambulance to take him to the hospital, the angel came back to Lori, retrieved his jacket, and said, "Please, have a beautiful day."

Given the circumstances, the statement could have sounded ridiculous and insensitive. But the man's presence was, well, beautiful. In that moment, he had given Lori everything she needed.

She turned away for a second to deal with John, and when she turned back to thank the man, he was gone.

Later, at the hospital, after John had been checked out and declared injury-free, Lori asked him, "If your angel could wear anything at all, what would it be?"

Without hesitation John said, "A Dodgers hat."

# 19

# Time to Take Another Chance

Because Batten disease is a progressive neurological disorder, we continually needed to adapt to a new normal. With the advance of the disease came new and more difficult challenges, and to meet them we needed to de-stress our lives as much as possible or give in to neurosis. (Lori sometimes thinks I chose the latter.)

Lori was doing a fantastic job caring for the boys, but her job became more demanding as they became more dependent, which is the opposite of how the mother-child relationship usually works. Adolescents crave independence as their capacity for it develops. My boys had the same desire for autonomy as other kids their age, but their minds and bodies would not allow them to have it. The gap between their desires and reality took a toll on all of us.

Sadly, my being a cop was taking a toll on the family too. When I donned my police uniform, I stood taller and felt stronger. And chasing bad guys, standing up to bullies, and providing protection to the community was very rewarding. But ten-hour shifts often stretched to sixteen hours or longer. When I punched the clock to check in, I never knew when I would be able to punch out, and my "days off" were sometimes taken up by court appearances. Police work is taxing for anyone, but for me, with two special-needs children at home, it was exacting too high a price. I did not have enough left over for Lori and the boys.

So we began to explore other possibilities. Financial security seemed important, but it was as elusive to us as everything else in our world. Youth was supposed to be a time of health and vigor, but not for our children. That reality focused Lori and me on the present moment—the only thing any of us really possesses—and the promised life to come. We weren't trying to be Aesop's irresponsible grasshopper, who plays around all summer, stores up nothing for the winter, and is saved from starvation by industrious and neighborly ants. But we really had no talent for planning ahead. Even though our perspective sustained us in our darkest hours, it did not give us the practical solutions we needed. Those solutions, however, arrived by a different route.

As we mulled over my options for another career path, our dear friend Bob Maurer, a clinical psychologist, suggested that I would make a good therapist. (Clearly, he had forgotten about the practical jokes I had played on him.)

"You have a natural curiosity about people and are a good listener," Bob said. "If you could tolerate a few more years in school, it could work. Take some time; think about it. Maybe you could take a class at a time."

I thought for about four minutes, talked to Lori for a couple more, and immediately enrolled in a full-time program for a master's degree in psychology. The thought that I would be able to take back some control over my time by changing my profession, coupled with my adventurous spirit, was all I needed to leap back into school. Although my being a full-time cop and a full-time student drove me even crazier than I already was and gave Lori more to do around the house, we both could see light at the end of the tunnel. I figured that in a couple of years, with my advanced degree in psychology, I would be a master psycho instead of just a regular one. No, seriously, both Lori and I could see that the long-term benefit of more family time was worth the short-term sacrifice.

Somehow our solution to not having enough time was to do more than we had been doing before. But the insane schedule was a means to an end, not an end in itself. Since we were already running from pillar to post—and still had my police salary, not to mention some room left on the credit cards—we decided to squeeze in some vacations too.

In the summer of 2004, John and I went to Alaska. The trip, which had been a dream of mine, was a birthday present to me from Lori and some of our friends. John and I landed in Juneau and stayed in a rustic place with a small kitchen. We didn't have a lot of money for eating out, so, for most of our meals, we got some essential guy food, such as frozen lasagna (which, men, is not supposed to be eaten frozen but tastes just fine that way too).

One of our most memorable experiences was riding on a dog sled. John would have been content just to hang out with the eighty barking, frolicking huskies, but when we were given the heavy jackets and gloves, he sensed adventure. Our guides must have forgotten to cover his mouth because his smile was frozen in place.

Once fourteen or so dogs were hooked up to a sled, John was seated comfortably inside it. Behind the musher, I was tethered to another sled and stood on the runners. The musher yelled something, John shouted and waved his arms, I gave the command (I think), and off we went.

Pulled by the loping dogs, we sailed around a mighty glacier. The air was crisp and chilly, but the excitement made us forget about the cold, except for trying to look cool by not falling off the sled. Midway through the ride, we stopped to take in the view. The space was so vast, it didn't appear that we had traveled far, but it would have taken all day to cover the same ground by walking. An hour later, we arrived back where we had started, and John spent more time playing with his furry friends.

To me the ride seemed the perfect metaphor for life. We do all this running around, yet in the grand scheme of things, how much important ground do we really cover? Eternity provides the best measure for the distance we need to travel, yet who could traverse that far? No one— that is, no one without God's help.

Later that year, Lori and I spent a few days together skiing on Mammoth Mountain, in the heart of the Sierra Nevada range. Time alone as a couple was rare, but needed. With so much of our attention and energy focused on John and Ben, it was important that we not lose sight of each other. But if we waited for an ideal moment to get away (such as when we could afford it), we never would get away. By connecting as a couple, and deepening our love, we had more love to give our children and more courage to face, together, whatever was to come.

# 20

# Love Made Perfect

John was winning hearts with his courageous spirit, but his own was broken. His friends' lives were expanding: dating, parties, plans for college. Keeping up with them was impossible. His strength was waning, and so was ours. We needed help—all of us.

At this moment, dear friends gave us a golden retriever puppy. As they say, every boy needs a puppy. (At least that's the myth perpetuated at the pet store.) What they don't say is that puppies like to chew. At first it's kind of cute. But when they start eating the legs on the piano, it's not so cute. The puppy's name was Saint, and he soon became known as Saint the Ferocious in some circles, and Satan in others. Let's just say that things got a bit out of hand.

We were fortunate to have other friends, the Feddersens, who raised puppies to prepare them for training as guide dogs for the blind. Patty Feddersen, God bless her, took Saint into her home to teach him some manners, such as not eating smaller dogs. But unfortunately, Saint never quite mastered canine etiquette. We loved Saint, sure, but we had started to worry that he was going to work his way up to eating small children. He had been a gift of perfect love, but he was not the perfect gift for us. And in the end, he had to go.

We found Saint a home with enough space for him to live out his, well, desire to eat things. But John and Ben lost it when the time came to take Saint there. I was at work, so poor Lori had to shoulder the task alone. Both boys yelled at her: "How could a mother do this to her boys, give away their dog?" At one point she had to pull off the freeway because tears were filling her eyes too. John never bonded as deeply with a dog again.

Saint's move to the country left a hole in the Sikorra home. I wouldn't say that dogs are *always* man's best friend. They often are, however, little boys' best friends. Longing for the play and the company that only a dog could provide, the boys often asked the Feddersens if Bessie, a black lab they had been training, could have a play day at our house.

Bessie had not made the grade in puppy training and had not been placed in guide-dog school. She had instead become the Feddersens' pet. Several months after Bessie started coming over to play with our boys, the Feddersens offered to give us their beloved dog. It was a generous offer, for Bessie had become a member of their family. She was born to be a helper, they told us, and she just might provide the kind of help we needed then. With deep gratitude, we accepted this gift of love. It was yet another instance when God, through His people, gave us a gift to let us know that He was there, that He cared.

In no time, Bessie was an integral part of our family. We toyed with the idea of getting her a harness so that we could bring her everywhere, but we decided against it. After all, she had flunked guide-dog preschool. She might not have been the perfect guide dog, but she did her new job—bringing comfort, joy, and laughter—perfectly.

So many people wanted to help us, to be generous, to be giving. But they didn't always know how. And we didn't always know what we needed. Even when we did, we didn't always know how to ask for it. We often felt awkward and at a loss for words.

Human love is imperfect, but it is the material God uses to give us His own perfect love. He takes the gifts we offer in love, whether they are large, small, or even misguided, and transforms them into His love. We Catholics believe that the same thing happens at Mass. We offer bread and wine along with our bruised and broken lives. God accepts our gifts and transforms them into Himself, which He then gives back to us so that we can become like Him.

We don't need to know how to love perfectly. We just need to love the best way we can and let God do the rest.

# 21

# Don't Know How This Will Work, Part 1

"The race doesn't always go to the fastest, but sometimes to the one who doesn't quit." So goes the lesson of Aesop's "The Tortoise and the Hare". John was our tortoise, our stellar example of steady perseverance in the face of enormous odds. And as Lori and I were about to give up on his formal education, given the condition of his mind and his body, John asked us to send him to a Catholic high school, where he could openly share his faith with others. Clearly, as far as John was concerned, the race was not done. He had hit a few walls, but walls were for climbing, right?

"Why can't I go to a Catholic school with my friends?" he asked.

A great question, and we weren't going to excuse ourselves from the effort of answering it by giving some lame reply. Excuses can be a way of escaping responsibility, and they can prevent us from becoming who we are meant to become. Excuses don't lead us anywhere but leave us where we are. They might feel good, but action that leads us forward feels better.

Besides, Lori and I still hoped that we could somehow fit in at a Catholic school, but hope absent action remains only a dream. "We need to ask questions, to explore the possibilities," Lori and I said to each other. "This is what John wants." Thus, we began to make inquiries about Catholic high schools in our area.

Of course, we had no money for tuition, but that was the least of our worries. John couldn't perform academically at a high school level. He couldn't read (not even braille) or write or solve math problems beyond the simplest of equations, much less do abstract reasoning. And due to his visual impairment, he would need full-time assistance.

Our friends the Griffins (the family that gave us Saint) arranged a meeting for us at Loyola, a boys' Jesuit high school near downtown Los Angeles. Given that Loyola is one of the premier college preparatory schools in Southern California, we were amazed that the administration was open to the idea of admitting John. There were insurmountable obstacles, however. The school was too far from home to allow us to get there quickly in the event of a medical emergency, and given the frequency of John's seizures, the risk that he would have an emergency was high. In addition, the principal wanted John to attend full-time, but Lori and I didn't think he could tolerate a full school day. By this time, he was weaker and needed more sleep. Even though Loyola proved not to be the right place for John, the willingness of the administration to consider John increased our hope, and we kept looking.

My friend Ross Porter, a psychologist, suggested Chaminade College Preparatory. "I used to teach there," Ross said. "They're good people. And we live right across the street, should something happen."

We went straight to the top and arranged a meeting with the principal, Brother Tom. "You see, we got kicked out of our Catholic grade school," I said almost as

soon as the meeting began. Probably not the best intro-
duction to our story, but I wanted Brother Tom to know
what our family had been through. Since he graciously
responded by getting comfortable in his chair, I could see
that the meeting wasn't going to be a normal admittance
interview.

Some of our story came with tears, because Lori and
I were still holding on to some of the anger and the sadness
we had felt when the Catholic grade school seemed to
have rejected John.

"What do you want Chaminade to do for John?" asked
Brother Tom.

"Love him. That's all," I replied.

"I don't know how this will work," Brother Tom said,
"but why don't we see?"

He took up John's application with the staff. No doubt
they too had their reservations. In their defense, there were
many practical reasons for them to say no. Making room
for John was entering uncharted territory. The easy answer
would have been, "Your son seems like a great kid. I'm
sorry we can't accommodate him, but you understand."

Brother Tom ran it by his boss, the president of the
school, Jim Adams. Jim's reply was along the lines of "Let's
not allow fear to prevent us from doing the right thing. If
we can serve John, we will."

John was enrolled, and Lori and I were amazed, asking:
How in the world is this going to work?

We hired an aide to help John go from class to class, to
pick him up when he fell, and to call if he had a seizure.
After going through a few aides who didn't work out, we
hit a home run when we found Cody Miller, who was
kind, bright, and just quirky enough for the job. Cody
was barely out of high school himself, making him more
relatable to the kids.

The previous spring, our local community (mostly folks from church) had done some fund-raising. The subsequent account was to be used for paying medical bills, providing opportunities for the boys, and taking care of various expenses. There wasn't enough money to cover four years of private high school, but there was enough to get John started. God had opened this door for John and had given us enough of a nudge to go through it. What would happen later, we decided to leave up to Him.

John looked great in his uniform. He usually wore a colored polo shirt and khaki shorts, which had a Velcro closure instead of a zipper and a button that he could no longer manage because of a decline in fine motor skills. If we set his clothes out for him, he had no difficulty dressing himself.

John wasn't afraid, and we tried to follow his example. And Brother Tom smoothed the way by meeting John at the front steps of the school pretty much every day during his freshman year.

"As long as Johnny is smiling, we'll keep going," Brother Tom said. "One day at a time."

John smiled. And smiled. And smiled. He fulfilled his desire to attend a school where he learned about his faith, prayed, *and* was surrounded by pretty girls.

He participated with the football team during his junior year as the personal hydration absorption specialist (aka water boy) for quarterback Ryan Griffin, his friend. Ryan later became a starting quarterback at Tulane University. After college he was drafted by the New Orleans Saints. We would like to think John's water had a lot to do with Ryan's football career. John beamed and waved to the approving crowd whenever his name was announced during a game. He was celebrated, and we cried tears of joy. John got it: no matter the experience, the role, it had value if it could be shared.

John's high school years brought Lori and me back into the mainstream somewhat. Friday-night football games, carpooling with other families—these ordinary aspects of raising teenagers felt really good. We found that we could fit in at a Catholic school after all.

## 22

# Don't Know How This Will Work,
# Part 2

During John's high school years, the time came for me to leave the police force. I had finished my master's degree in psychology and had begun interning as a therapist.

"Well, let's see," I reasoned with Lori. "We're broke, but that isn't new. I have about two low-fee clients, with no future guarantees of a better income. So let's go for it."

To make things easier on the financial front, Lori volunteered to return to part-time work as a nurse, which would also provide the family with medical insurance. She didn't want to go back into the workforce, but she was willing to do so for me. Her love and support continued to amaze me.

The police job had served me and my family beautifully. It had provided financial security for about seven years, which had gotten us through some tough times, and as a bonus it had given me some tremendous life experience that would serve me well as a therapist.

As a police officer, I often dealt with people in crisis: they were depressed and wanted to die. They were fighting with their spouses, and their marriages were falling apart. They had experienced traumatic injuries and losses. They struggled with addictions and other self-destructive behaviors. As a therapist, I would deal with the same issues, but with one big difference: I would not be able to lock up the suffering in jail. In fact, my job would be geared toward unlocking the emotional and the psychological jail people had created for themselves or had found themselves in, and helping them to free themselves.

There was another significant difference. As a cop, I frequently found myself in the position of telling people what to do: "Stop! Put your hands up!" While people frequently ask their therapists to tell them what to do, therapists must resist the temptation to do so. Telling people what to do is not therapeutic. To walk with people through their pain and struggle so that they can see for themselves the path they should take, to listen to them so that they can hear their own insights—that is the job of a therapist. Telling people what to do is the opposite of empowering them, and it robs them of the joy they could experience from self-discovery and taking responsibility for their lives and their achievements.

I hung my uniform in my locker for the last time on November 18, 2007, and I unloaded my big H&K .45 (and a few other guns). These were not only deadly weapons, but symbols of persuasion by force. Force can challenge behavior, even stop behavior, but it cannot change a heart for the better. That inner transformation requires freedom.

This is not to say that I was not a force for good as a police officer. I would like to think that I was. We feel best about ourselves when we believe that our jobs, and our very existence, are making a positive difference—not just in our lives but in the lives of others. "Making a difference" is something we all yearn to do.

As a policeman, I certainly hadn't changed the world. I hadn't even tried to, for that would have been a crazy aspiration. But had I changed my community? Hard to say. Maybe in a small way I had made a positive impact on a few lives. On the home front I had made a contribution.

My wife and my sons were proud of me, and Lori was grateful for the sacrifice that gave her more time at home with the boys.

There was a dark side to the job, however. People say cops are cold and detached. (Those are some of the politer terms people use.) And they are not far from the mark. The police witness so much brutality, that they must distance themselves emotionally from their work so that they can remain integrated with their off-duty lives. If they take in too much of the viciousness around them, they can become demoralized, or worse. Sad but true, in hardening themselves to the horrors of the job, a part of their humanity dies. I experienced this phenomenon myself.

The same thing happens to other professionals who witness violence or intense suffering—soldiers, firefighters, doctors, and even social workers can attest to the toll their jobs take on their psyches and their families. Yet these roles are important because everyone depends on them, which is why they are honorable professions.

The word "vocation" comes from the Latin verb that means "to call". We use the word to refer to a call from the Lord to serve others. I believe that I had indeed been called by the Lord to serve my family and my community as a police officer. But after several years, the toughening that the police role required conflicted with the attentiveness that my family needed. So another calling made itself heard. As a therapist, my mission to serve would remain. The mission field is what would change.

As I made the transition to being a therapist, I felt as if I were a lump of clay being remolded by God, yet again. And I soon discovered that I would have more to learn in my new profession than I had anticipated.

At first I would tell my new clients, in an effort to reassure them, that I had been a cop, that nothing they could say would shock me. I was a rookie. I didn't realize it was a naïve and insensitive thing to say. One day, however, a client told me about her grandparents who worshipped the devil and practiced cannibalism. Yes, I was a little shocked, and I had to admit that on the Santa Monica police force, I had not seen or heard it all.

# 23

# Risk, Purpose, and Meaning

I was taking Bessie for a walk one typical winter day in Southern California; the temperature was in the low 60s. Compared with most other places in the country at that time of year, it was not cold at all. So when I looked across the park and saw a dog wearing a cute little sweater, I laughed out loud. I wanted to shout, "Take off the sweater, my little furry friend, and feel the snap in the air. Take the risk to be who you are."

Perhaps the critter was returning from the doggie beauty salon and didn't have enough of its natural coat left to keep out the cold. Or perhaps the dog's owner was projecting her fear of discomfort, or her need to make a fashion statement, on her pet. Either way, the scene seemed absurd because dogs were designed to live outdoors. And besides, I thought to myself, our best lessons are learned when we are uncomfortable.

In our younger years, so many of us feel bulletproof. Confident of our invulnerability, we boldly plunge into dangerous situations. As a teenager, I skied in alligator-infested lakes just for pleasure. As a young man, I gave up steady employment to pursue an acting career. I did stunt shows at Universal Studios during my acting days, and although I was a trained professional, I would push the envelope to make the stunt a little more spectacular. Some of the other stunt people I knew got seriously injured in their line of work. Yet I still believed that disaster would never strike me.

But why was I taking these risks? What was the pay-off? Risk without purpose, without God's purpose, is just recklessness. Yet I was wired for adventure. It took me a while to learn how these things go together.

God indeed has a plan for us, and it is beyond anything we could ever dream up for ourselves. When we give our desires to Him and trust Him to guide us, He leads us on an amazing adventure that fulfills our deepest longings.

From the time she was a girl, Mother Teresa of Calcutta wanted to be a missionary in India. She joined a religious order with schools there, and she became a teacher in one of them. After some years, she left her teaching job and moved into a Calcutta slum. She didn't risk her health and safety for a thrill. She heard God calling her to care for the poorest of the poor. She pushed herself even further outside her comfort zone to say yes to God.

In the parable of the talents, Jesus teaches us not to play it safe. A master gave one of his servants five talents to invest, the parable tells us. The servant took the talents and doubled them. Another servant received two talents. He also doubled the master's money. Both men took risks to achieve their goals. But the third servant, who was given one talent, was fearful and resentful of his master. He dared not even try investing the coin but buried it in the ground. In the end, the master took the talent away from the fearful servant and gave it to the one who had ten.

The master, who represents God, gave the coins to His servants so that the servants could fulfill *His* purpose, and fulfilling God's purpose is what fulfills us. Who among us wants to be a coward who does nothing worthwhile because he fears taking risks? God gives us one life to live, and fear alone stands between us and our glorious destiny.

John and Ben taught me how to take risks so that we could live as children of God. Batten disease robbed them of some of their natural abilities, but not of their desire to use whatever they had to participate fully in life.

John wanted to be an altar boy, what he called a "Holy Boy". And so, with the help of other altar servers, he carried the gifts and rang the bells. Surely God must have smiled as John fearlessly offered whatever he had to serve Him with such love and devotion. Of course, his mother and I were very proud of him. But we were also nervous wrecks, waiting for him to trip, to fall off the steps, or to have a seizure during the Consecration. But those were our fears. We wanted to put a sweater on him, as that woman I had seen put a sweater on her dog.

Ben also responded to the call. He began to assist the ushers with taking up the collection during Mass. Occasionally he would knock people in the head with the basket, but he was so proud of his ministry.

One Sunday after Mass, Ben asked, "Dad, do you think Jesus is really happy that I'm helping Him?"

"I think all the angels rejoice in your service."

"So does that mean Jesus is happy?"

"Yup."

The boys tried to cultivate other abilities. When John turned sixteen, he wanted to drive. This desire was simply an age-appropriate want—all his friends were learning to drive—but I did not have the heart to say no when he had the guts to try the impossible.

I drove him to an off-road facility in my four-wheel-drive Jeep Wrangler, while Lori stayed home and maintained a prayer vigil. Lots of dirt roads and few cars, and John did great, considering his limitations.

"A little left, John. A little right. Slower. SLOWER! LOOK OUT FOR THAT—"

*Crunch.*

"Cactus."

Moving forward again, I spotted some motorcycle riders in the distance. They had just crested a giant dirt hill we were preparing to ascend.

"John, stop the car! Now!"

"Which pedal again?"

"STOP!"

He slammed on the brakes, and a cloud of dust billowed up from the ground and surrounded us. I got out of the Jeep as quickly as possible and stood outside the driver's door. I didn't have time to move John into the passenger seat.

When the motorcycle riders stopped next to us, just to be friendly, I realized that they were several cops I used to work with at the Santa Monica Police Department. How was I going to explain what I was doing? I couldn't say, "Oh, hello. Nice day. Just teaching my blind son how to drive."

After some meaningless and forgettable jiving, my former colleagues moved on. Needless to say, the driving lesson was over.

John went home with a big smile, but he soon realized that he was never going to drive the way his friends did. There were lots of things they were doing that he would never be able to do. Sometimes when he compared himself with others, he felt sad or angry. Comparison plays that nasty trick on all of us.

There are always people who have more than we do and people who have less. When we compare ourselves with those who have more, we feel worse about ourselves. And when we look at others worse off, we rather shamefully feel better about ourselves. Sometimes, to feel better about ourselves, we even manufacture negative things about other people. The solution to the pitfalls of comparison is to give thanks for the blessings we possess *and* to have gratitude for the blessings of others.

For the most part, John's grateful heart gave him wonderful perspective. Once I heard him say, "I'm so excited that I could see really good when I was five and six."

"And it kills me that you can't now," I wanted to say.

He was, by far, the bigger man at that moment. He was bigger by being willing to be smaller.

Jesus told us that unless we become like children, we cannot enter His kingdom.

How are we to be like them? By trusting and accepting.

Reckless behavior can be indicative of an unconscious death wish, and yet inaction is an unconscious fear of living, which leads to the death of the soul. Our fulfillment is realized somewhere in between, in the place where we dream big, desire greatness, and give all to God so that we might fulfill His purposes for us.

## 24

# Remember, Life Is But a Whisper

My family loved Bessie dearly. She helped us transition to a simpler life. As the boys' physical capabilities slowed, she took up the slack. John and Ben did less running on the beach, so she did it for them. They laughed and cheered her on as she chased birds, although we all suspected that she wouldn't know what to do with a bird if she caught one.

One day, she proved our hunch. Seeing a pesky crow sitting on the front lawn, she ran out the door and gave chase. Before the bird could gain altitude, it flew into a wall and was momentarily stunned. Bessie came to a screeching halt several feet from the grounded bird, barked once, then turned in terror toward the house.

After only two years with us, Bessie developed a limp. Lori and the boys took her to the vet and left her there for an exam. It was the last time they saw her alive. On the examining table, she had what the vet thought was a heart attack and died. Despite his considerable efforts, he was unable to revive her.

Bravely, Lori took the boys to the clinic so that they could say their good-byes. They all held Bessie and cried. Toward the end of the workday, Lori called me to pass along the sad news.

"Dr. Bodie is staying at the clinic until you can see her," she said.

Our dear vet's sensitivity to our family, including its four-legged members, was much appreciated. When I arrived at the clinic about 10:00 P.M., he led me into the small room where Bessie was laid out. I held her in my arms and cried. A door had opened that I could not shut. I don't think I was crying only for Bessie.

"Do you think dogs go to heaven?" I asked Dr. Bodie. "Will I see her again?"

Perhaps this was a question for a theologian or a clergyman. But at this moment, Dr. Bodie, with his deep connection to animals, seemed the best person to ask. I don't remember his exact answer, but he spoke of God's love and mercy and the fact that animals were His creation too. The response didn't stop the tears, but it brought a measure of comfort.

I went home, and not surprisingly, I found the family still awake, sitting on the couch or lying on the floor. Through the tears, the questions flowed: "Will we see Bessie again, Dad?" "What happened?" "Why did she have to die?"

Remembering Dr. Bodie's words, I answered, "Dogs are God's creation too. They are part of His plan." My understanding didn't go much further than that. So we clung to each other, shared our sorrow, and after a while, exhausted, fell asleep.

Hope is essential for coping with loss and grief. It is not our intellectual understanding that sustains us through difficulty, but our trust that Someone far bigger than we are has the whole world in His hands.

We were already dealing with a lot of loss in our lives. And Bessie's sudden death added to that burden. Yet our grief taught us a valuable lesson. "Blessed are those who mourn, for they shall be comforted" (Mt 5:4). Whenever we feel sad at the passing of a beloved person, or even a special pet, we realize that something is wrong with the world. Somehow we know that life is meant to go on forever. So why doesn't it?

It does, but not here. And so we learn to hold on less tightly with the expectation that something even better awaits us in the world to come.

Bessie was irreplaceable. Her personality and the contribution she made to our household were unique. But after a few months we realized that we needed another dog, for the joy it could bring to our family and the calming effect it could have on Ben. Funny that a dog could do for Ben what no person seemed able to accomplish.

We talked to friends, particularly our dog-lover friends. We had learned (the hard way with Saint) that no ordinary dog would do. We needed a mature dog, with some manners, and maybe even sensitivity to the blind. A tall order? Well, we weren't given everything we wished for, but we got more than what we thought we could reasonably expect.

Again through our friends the Feddersens, we made contact with some good folks at Guide Dogs of America, the wonderful organization that provides training for both dogs and their blind companions. Their "rejects" had worked really well for us in the past. After a lot of searching, they came up with a possible dog for us to adopt.

"Her name is Fumi, but she has a couple of issues," they said.

Yeah, such as her name, for starters, I thought. Fumi sounds like an awful-tasting mushroom used to support colon health. But, as with most of my goofy thoughts, I wisely chose not to share this one.

"Oh? What kind of issues?" we asked.

"Well, reportedly, she's a counter thief. Her owner had some problems with her stealing food from the table."

I can imagine that a food-stealing dog would be a little frustrating. Her blind companion makes a nice meal for himself, and his "helper" sneaks up and helps herself to it. "Although we tried to set her up, she wouldn't steal any food from us when we took her back. She knows we can see her, and she refrains. But when she goes back to her owner, it's another story."

Since at least half of those in our house could see, we thought this canine kleptomaniac wouldn't present too big a problem. Boy, were we wrong. Within days of coming to our home, Fumi helped herself to a loaf of bread we left on the counter. But remembering one of my favorite books, *Les Miserables*, and the hero who is imprisoned after stealing a loaf of bread for his sister's starving family, how could I condemn my poor dog? Later, though, when she turned her thievery on my steak, the crime was far more difficult to forgive. Yet we still fell in love with Fumi and chose to keep her.

The name, however, would have to go, we agreed. The kids couldn't remember it.

"Here, Frumpy."

"Fuji, put that down!"

"Dad, Fruffy stole my shoe!"

I think even the dog was getting confused.

After looking into dog names and how to help a dog to recognize a new one, we settled on the name Lily. Ben chose it. She had a beautiful face and a sweet disposition in spite of her food-stealing habit.

Lily had another defect. She did not particularly like going on walks—probably not the best trait for a guide dog. But with time, we came to see that she had a calling. In crazy small ways, she became more of a life guide, reminding us—me—about some important truths.

Dogs are oftentimes more faithful than we are. We can forget to feed them, but they don't hold grudges; we can ignore them when we come home, but, chances are, they'll still greet us the next time with equal enthusiasm; we can forget to take them out, and—well, that's not a great example. They seem to believe, to trust, to forgive.

Sure, Lily had her quirks, but we were not perfect ourselves. And strangely, as we discovered, perfect love doesn't require perfection. In fact, perfect love requires the acceptance of imperfection.

Imperfection and mortality—these are the causes of our losses. And mourning them with acceptance and hope is the gateway to eternal life.

# 25

# Pay Attention

I invited some friends over to celebrate my birthday. The backyard was full, and everyone was having fun. Many people were standing beside the pool, but nobody was really paying attention to the swimmers.

Lori was gardening, two feet away from the pool, when the Spirit spoke to her: "Put the clippers down. You're not paying attention."

The voice, she said, was as clear as can be. It spoke to her mind and her heart, not her ears. She obeyed and turned. As she did, she saw John having a seizure and sinking to the bottom of the pool. Immediately she dove in and pulled him to the side. I was called from the front yard, and I carried John into the living room. He had stopped seizing and appeared all right, but we called the paramedics anyway. (As God would have it, our house was about two minutes from a fire station.)

John recovered particularly quickly, perhaps because the television was on and he heard the voice of Vin Scully calling the Dodgers game. Nothing grabs John's attention more than Vin and the Dodgers. Lori and I recovered less quickly. Lori felt particularly shaken. It had been a close call.

The next day, Lori went for her favorite walk in Malibu at the Serra Retreat Center. Its twenty-three acres sit atop a knoll between the Santa Monica Mountains and the Pacific Ocean. Its gardens with sweeping views create an ideal place to recollect oneself.

"Lord, I cannot do this," Lori prayed. "Mary, how did you do it? How did you watch your Son suffer and die? Give me courage. Give me strength as a mother."

There are voices inside us all. (And I'm not speaking about the schizophrenic kind.) Some call these voices self-talk. They say that "tapes" formed during our upbringing replay inside our heads for the rest of our lives. If we grow up with people who love us and affirm us, these tapes can encourage us when life is tough. If we grow up with neglect, abuse, or lots of criticism, we can develop an inner critic who always finds fault and tells us that we do not deserve to be loved.

God's voice, on the other hand, is not one of these tapes. He tells us that we are wonderfully made by Him, for His good purpose. Yes, we are flawed and at times rebellious. But He never stops calling us back to our true selves—to act justly, to love freely, and to walk humbly as we place our trust in Him.

"Listen to me," God says. "You'll have all you need and so much more."

God speaks to us all. Whether we hear Him depends on whether we are paying attention.

But back to Lori's prayers. One way God answered them was with a phone call.

"Mr. Sikorra?" said the voice on the other end of the phone.

"God?"

"No. This is so-and-so [not her real name] from Pennsylvania. Someone from your community wants to send your family to Medjugorje. They want to remain anonymous."

I thought for a moment that we were being kicked out of Westlake and sent to some unknown land. I didn't know much about the place.

The woman explained that we were being invited on a pilgrimage to a place of prayer and healing.

"Great. We'll pack."

Getting away sounded great, healing would be wonderful, and we could all do a little more praying. Lori and I felt the now familiar sense of wonder and gratitude that hit us each time we experienced such a generous gift of love. As the donor wanted to remain anonymous, there was little we could do but accept the gift and prepare for yet another God adventure. We flew off to the former Yugoslavia not knowing what to expect, but knowing that the unexpected often turned out wonderful.

Medjugorje is a small village in Bosnia–Herzegovina. Its name means "between mountains". I would describe the landscape as similar to Southern California without the congestion and the decades of urban development—a beautiful land of beautiful people.

When we arrived, we all felt a little restless. Truth be told, we weren't very good at saying the Rosary. And the Rosary is one of the main events in Medjugorje. Jet-lagged, displaced, and unable to find a Starbucks, I took a walk through some vineyards while the rest of the family took a nap. As I strolled, I began to pray, and some Scripture verses came to mind.

The first one was "Blessed are those who have not seen and yet believe" (Jn 20:29), the words the risen Jesus spoke to doubting Thomas. I thought of a couple of possible meanings these words might have for our family. For one thing, our boys couldn't see, literally, but they believed. Were they blessed? It wasn't the blindness, per se, that made them blessed, but their believing hearts.

Perhaps God was preparing me for the miracles I would and *would not* see in Medjugorje. We Christians are encouraged to pray for the things we want. And when we get the really big things, we usually call it a miracle. When we get everything else we *really need*—life, breath, love, and so on—we call that just another day.

God's ways are not always our ways. How would my life have been different if I had received fame and fortune as an actor? Would I have been a better man or a worse one? It's hard to say for sure, but I don't think the struggle, the pain, and the sacrifice have been bad for me. That's why "Your will be done, Lord" is always the most necessary thing to include in any prayer. God knows best what miracles we truly need. Those who believe in God's care for them even when their prayers seem to go unanswered, those who simply trust God and place themselves at His disposal, are truly blessed.

The next words I heard were "They follow me because I fed them" and "Seek me, not the miracles." These are similar to the words that Jesus said after multiplying the loaves and the fish. When crowds of people began following Jesus, He said to them, "You seek me, not because you saw signs, but because you ate your fill of the loaves. Do not labor for the food which perishes, but for the food which endures to eternal life, which the Son of man will give to you" (Jn 6:26–27).

Lori and I, and everyone praying for our family, would have been overjoyed to see the boys cured of Batten disease, to see their vision and health restored. And surely such a miracle would have given glory to God. Yet the Lord seemed to be telling me that our desire for a miraculous cure was a distraction from what truly mattered. To know that God was present and cared—as John had told us years earlier—to trust God so much that we could say yes to whatever He asked of us: that's what really mattered.

A couple of days into the trip, Lori explored the cost of escaping from Medjugorje. We both felt a bit panicky. It was hard to go from the thriving metropolis of Los Angeles to a little a town where visitors are promised plenty of time to pray and pray. To pray that much requires letting go of goals and of all sorts of activities. God speaks to us in silence. His still, small voice is like the whisper of a quiet breeze. If you're living inside a tornado, it's easy to miss.

"How much to go to Dubrovnik?" Lori asked a travel agent.

Dubrovnik is a gorgeous historic city on the Mediterranean coast of Croatia. Luckily, we couldn't afford the detour. We were forced to stay put. And as the days progressed, we fell into a peaceful rhythm of daily Mass, prayer, and rest. (And cold beer and pizza at night.) Even Energy Boy Ben acquired a spirit of contentment.

One particularly memorable day, we walked up Apparition Hill. The climb wasn't pleasant. The hill's jagged red and gray rocks make it a challenge for even the surefooted, never mind the elderly or the blind. But climbing the hill isn't about getting somewhere. It's about going somewhere. A journey up. A journey in.

It was here that Mary, the Mother of Jesus, first allegedly appeared to several of the town's children. More than twenty years later, some of the visionaries claim to see her daily. In her messages, they say, Mary points to her Son, Jesus, the Redeemer through whom we receive everlasting life.

We also tackled Cross Mountain, a brutal hike, due (again) to the jagged rocks. Making their way to the top, visitors encounter Stations of the Cross, where they can recount the Passion of Jesus. Near the top of the hill stands a large concrete cross built in 1934.

It was not uncommon to see pilgrims, even elderly ones, walking up the hill barefoot. We saw others, those unable to walk, carried by the able-bodied and the stouthearted. It occurred to me that the path through life is often rocky, and God does not intend for us to walk it alone.

The hike up Cross Mountain was particularly difficult for my boys, as they couldn't see the rocks and where to step. Lori and I each took a boy's hand and slowly picked our way around and over the rocks. We had to watch not only our every step but also each step of the boys so that no one would trip or sprain an ankle. Once at the top, we rested at the foot of the cross. How does God guide us? I wondered. The same way Lori and I just guided our sons up this mountain? How often do we resist this kind of help from God?

The trip down the hill proved even more difficult. I alternately carried John or Ben on my back, while Lori supported the other. In the difficulty of the descent, the boys leaned on Lori and me even more. We went along hand in hand and body against body for strength and balance. The difficult path brought us together in a way that no smooth path ever could. Sore muscles were a small price to pay for that closeness.

One evening, we had the good fortune of meeting with one of the people who claimed to see Mary on special occasions. The middle-aged woman was simple and friendly. After she spoke to our group about Mary's messages, Ben raised his hand at question-and-answer time.

"The next time you see Mary," he said, "tell her she wears too much perfume."

"Oh, boy," I thought. "Where is Ben going with this?" Ben was bold and prone to saying outrageous things. But profound things came out of his mouth too. Not knowing whether I should let him speak or tell him to be quiet, I thought about yelling, "Fire!", faking a heart attack, or pouring the bowl of lemonade on my head to distract attention from him.

But I was too late. The woman looked at Ben with intense interest, and he continued.

"She flew over to me when I was in front of the church, and she about knocked me over with her perfume."

"Tell me more," the woman said, taking a seat next to Ben.

"Well, she flew over to me. Why don't her feet ever touch the ground?"

The woman then asked Ben to describe Mary.

"She's little, with brown hair, brown eyes, and wears a gray dress, and her feet never touch the ground. She flies everywhere," Ben said. "She's a tiny lady. And I smelled her, her perfume. She smells like roses."

If we had pictures or statues of Mary around, perhaps it would have made sense that Ben described her as he did. But we didn't. (Not to mention that Ben was blind and couldn't really see *anyone*.) Even more curious, Ben is the product of public schools, which are certainly not known for their religious icons.

He went on to say that she didn't speak to him but came near and looked into his eyes. If Ben were contriving the story, he probably would have said that Mary wanted him to have more ice cream or a new guitar. But he said none of that. She just presented herself to him, he said.

As Lori's initial restlessness began to subside, she also heard messages—not a voice from the clouds, but God speaking quietly to her heart.

On one of our last evenings, we had been walking and praying, and John was getting tired. Lori led him near a statue of Jesus and made him comfortable on a bench. He began to doze, so Lori walked to some of the Stations of the Cross. At station ten, where Jesus is dying on the Cross, she realized that her life, her pain, couldn't compare with Mary's. John and Ben might die prematurely, but they wouldn't have nails deliberately driven through their hands and feet. What is more, they wouldn't be abandoned; they would be surrounded by love.

Lori walked to station four, where Simon of Cyrene is forced to help Jesus carry His Cross. The warm sun had set behind the mountains surrounding Medjugorje. The light was fading, but Lori's eyes were being opened.

"Please, God," she prayed, "let John and Ben always have friends to help them carry their cross."

The next day, Lori visited a refugee camp outside the city. There she met a mother carrying her seven-year-old boy in her arms. He was blind and had feeding tubes, but he was wearing new socks and clean clothes. He resembled children stricken with infantile Batten disease.

"I have a five-day-old baby inside," she told Lori. "Would you like to meet her?"

Lori's face lit up, and the women led her inside a hut. Lori held the infant, and the child's mother and father smiled proudly.

As Lori looked around, she was humbled and amazed. The hut had dirt floors, a cardboard roof, and neither electricity nor running water. The family of four shared one bed, but it was neatly made. The dishes were washed, and the place appeared cared for with grateful hands.

Again, Lori prayed. "Please, God, forgive me for my self-centeredness and pride. Help me to live simply and humbly."

On our last evening in Medjugorje, we had a jaw-dropping send-off. As if on cue, hundreds of people all turned, gasped, and pointed. The sun appeared to be spinning and pulsing as it glowed warmly. We all watched as it sank closer to the horizon. Medjugorje has a reputation for this phenomenon, which countless pilgrims have claimed to have seen. Not being a scientist, a doctor, or a theologian, I have no explanation for what I saw. I can only record my experience and leave it to the experts to explain it.

In 1991 the bishops' conference of the former Yugoslavia declared, "On the basis of the investigations so far it cannot be affirmed that one is dealing with supernatural apparitions and revelations [in Medjugorje]." Ever since, this statement has been repeated by the Vatican, which as of this writing has neither approved nor disapproved the claim that Mary has appeared to visionaries in Medjugorje. Regardless of what the Vatican ultimately decides about Medjugorje, my family returned home changed for the better.

First of all, we had learned how to pray. Oh, we had talked to God before, but we had not known how to listen. In Medjugorje, we discovered that we need to shut off the external and internal noise in order to hear the Spirit speak (still not an easy thing to do in Los Angeles).

Secondly, Lori had identified with Mary. They were both mothers facing the suffering and death of their sons, she realized. They understood each other's pain.

"Guide me, Mary," Lori prayed once we were home. "Do I continue to pray for healing for my little boys?" She wasn't ready to let go.

The answer came to her, but not the one she wanted: "You have to let God have your boys. Let God's will be done."

Lori cried. She couldn't imagine her life without them. Yet she trusted more completely than before that she would be given the strength to fulfill the mission God had given her.

# 26

# Pay Attention—Again!

When my birthday came around again, we decided to celebrate at Zuma Beach. We chose a somewhat remote spot where few people lay their towels and where there are no lifeguards. California beaches are very different from the beaches in Florida, where Lori and I grew up. The California Current goes from north to south along the California coast, and the water is cool (cold, Lori would say) even in the summer. The Florida Current goes in the opposite direction and delivers warm water along the Florida coast all year round. In addition to the colder water, rougher surf also makes California beaches less friendly than Florida ones. In spite of our backgrounds, or maybe because of them, Lori and I always felt a little intimidated whenever we took our boys to a California beach.

John always wore a life jacket when going into the ocean in case he had a seizure. So far, Ben had experienced only a couple of seizures, so we weren't quite as strict about making him wear one.

The boys took turns in the water: John first, then Ben. I stayed out in the surf, helping each boy catch waves on his boogie board. Lori stayed closer to shore to catch them and to point them back out to me to repeat the cycle. We were all having a great time.

Before Ben's next turn, Lori told him to put on a life jacket. Ben protested vehemently. We didn't make him wear it the first time he went in, after all. But a mother's intuition is often right, and Lori was adamant.

"You don't go in without it," she said.

Ben finally consented, and once again we were enjoying ourselves. I helped Ben catch a big wave, and he rode it beautifully toward the shore. After Lori turned him around, he slowly began to fight his way through the surf back out toward the sound of my voice. Suddenly, his face dropped into the water. Luckily, because he was wearing the jacket, he remained visible and afloat. Lori yelled at about the same time I saw him. We both converged as fast as we could, fighting against the surf. I don't know if it was my cop training that kept me calm or a strong sense of purpose and urgency to get to my son. In that moment, he was the only thing that mattered.

Lori reached him first, turned him over, and found him blue and still seizing. Fortunately, because his body was seizing, he wasn't sucking in seawater. We pulled him to the shore, and Lori called for paramedics.

Ben came to and fought to stay at the beach. He was having fun. Though somewhat incoherent, he knew what he wanted. He didn't know how precarious his situation had been just moments ago, and he didn't understand why he needed to be checked out at the hospital. But Ben's job wasn't to make good decisions that day. That was his parents' job. Ben wanted to live fully, to experience life on his terms. Bravo for him. It was our duty—Lori's and mine—to keep him alive.

How often are we in similar situations? Unaware of the danger, not realizing the stakes, we fight to have our way. We don't always know what's best for us, so we must listen to the One who does.

"I know what you want," I imagine God saying to me, "but I know better what you *need*. Obey."

I rode in the ambulance with Ben while Lori and John followed in the car. With lights flashing and siren blaring, we made our way from Zuma Beach to the local hospital. Another time, it would have been a beautiful ride, but our sadness and anxiety darkened the sky and cast a gray shadow upon the mountains. We were surrounded by majesty, but averted tragedy permeated the air.

The paramedics struggled with Ben to put the oxygen mask on his face. He was angry and disoriented—not a great combination, especially for Ben.

"Look, Ben," I said. "I'll do it."

I took a deep breath of bottled air from the mask, but since Ben seemed to be breathing fine, he won that fight. It was an expensive defeat for me, as I learned later from the bill. While the air we breathe all around us is free, the stuff in the bottle is not!

In the emergency room, Ben checked out okay. He even stopped resisting as he began to have a bit of fun with all the attention. He was in such high spirits as we left the hospital that he wanted to go back to the beach or to swim in the pool at home.

"How about a burger and a coke?" I said to change the subject.

Fortunately, Ben was hungry enough to accept food in place of adventure.

## 27

# A Tragic Loss

Lori and I lived with the pain of losing our boys from the time they were diagnosed with Batten disease. As the years of their childhood went by, the cross didn't get lighter, but the resistance made us stronger. Along the way, with much support and a lot of grace, a certain acceptance and peace accompanied us on the journey. Some parents, such as Kay and Brent Clark, are not given this gift of time.

Lori met Kay at Mommy and Me classes. Even after our children outgrew the program, we continued our friendship with the Clark family. One December morning when I answered the telephone, I heard a cry, then Kay's voice.

"Oh, my God! It's so terrible! It's so terrible! Cameron is dead!"

"What?" I asked incredulously.

"He killed himself. This morning. The police are just leaving."

Kay was given no time to prepare her heart for the loss of her son. She was in a state of shock and disbelief, and so was I. We had shared our faith and our struggles with raising children, but nothing could have prepared me for Cameron's decision to take his life.

Lori was at work, and I had no idea how to tell her—or my boys—this horrible news. Cameron was like a son to me and Lori and like a brother to John and Ben. I could think of no soft landing; I could only tell them the hard, unvarnished truth.

I picked up Lori, and we drove immediately to Kay and Brent's house, where we collapsed into each other's arms.

"Why? Why?" we kept asking through our tears. And none of us had any answers.

As relatives and other friends began to arrive, Lori and I went home to fetch our boys. We all needed to be there for Kay and Brent. We were family.

Ben couldn't stop crying, wailing. John, however, didn't break down. He was sad, but quiet. Meanwhile, Lori and I could not stop shaking our heads. For years, we had anticipated the premature deaths of John and Ben. We had imagined that our dear friends, including Cameron, would attend their funerals and mourn with us. Cameron wasn't supposed to die first.

The morning of Cameron's funeral Mass in Ventura was rainy. The large church was filled beyond capacity. Many kids from Cameron's high school had taken the day off to attend the service.

Brent addressed the congregation and shared stories of Cameron paddling out into ten-foot surf, flying down bike jumps in the hills of Ventura, and seeking adventure everywhere. Everyone in the church nodded and laughed. We had all witnessed such antics at one time or another and had our own stories to tell.

Catherine, fifteen, read a poem she had written entitled "Lost at Sea".

> How long you've been steering,
> The ship that I sail,
> So strong I've been holding
> The love in your trail.

The winds are still blowing,
My sails still held high
But with you lost at sea
My spirit can't fly

My heart has erupted
And there's a leak in my ship
They all try so hard
But they can't fix it.
The stitches won't hold
Because the only glue
Was the love and acceptance
That held me to you.

My ship started sinking
And hugs just won't do,
Because the only thing I want to feel
Is the hug that's from you.

Eleven-year-old Isabelle, Cameron's sister, read Lamentations 3:19–26:

Remember my affliction and my bitterness,
    the wormwood and the gall!
My soul continually thinks of it
    and is bowed down within me.
But this I call to mind,
    and therefore I have hope:
The steadfast love of the LORD never ceases,
    his mercies never come to an end;
they are new every morning;
    great is your faithfulness.
"The LORD is my portion," says my soul,
    "therefore I will hope in him."

The LORD is good to those who wait for him,
    to the soul that seeks him.
It is good that one should wait quietly
    for the salvation of the LORD.

The poem and the Old Testament reading captured
the emotion felt by all, but even these words fell short in
describing the depth of the pain everyone was experiencing,
especially the family. Then Cameron's uncle Jim read
from the Gospel of John, where Jesus wept at the tomb
of His friend Lazarus. Jesus felt the same grief we feel over
such a loss. He understands. But the story doesn't end
with death.

> Martha said to Jesus, "Lord, if you had been here, my
> brother would not have died. And even now I know that
> whatever you ask from God, God will give you." Jesus said
> to her, "Your brother will rise again." Martha said to him,
> "I know that he will rise again in the resurrection at the last
> day." Jesus said to her, "I am the resurrection and the life;
> he who believes in me, though he die, yet shall he live, and
> whoever lives and believes in me shall never die. Do you
> believe this?" She said to him, "Yes, Lord; I believe that
> you are the Christ, the Son of God, he who is coming into
> the world." (11:21–27)

None of us knew why Cameron—so full of exuberance,
so blessed with a loving and supportive family—took
his life. But we knew that Jesus had promised eternal life to
those who believe in Him. So we commended Cameron
to God with our prayers and our hope in His mercy.

Cameron's friends from high school were the pallbearers,
and John was among them. Wearing dark glasses,
they solemnly carried the casket into the church. The
dark glasses didn't really matter to John. He couldn't see

anyway. Although deeply grieved, John was different from the other kids in another respect: he smiled. For anyone else, that would have appeared inappropriate. But John, with one foot already in the next life, *knew* something the others doubted.

Ben, on the other hand, grieved Cameron for several years. He would sob and ask, "Why? Why did Cameron kill himself?" We couldn't give Ben an answer. Cameron left only questions. But surely he had been in a painful darkness that none of us had even guessed at.

We often wish we have better answers to life's tough questions. But sometimes the best we can offer is our empathy and our prayers. This truth was expressed beautifully in one of the songs the Clarks chose for Cameron's funeral: "The Servant Song" by Richard Gillard. The fourth verse goes as follows:

> I will weep when you are weeping
> When you laugh, I'll laugh with you
> I will share your joy and sorrow
> Till we've seen this journey through.

We gave Ben and our friends the Clarks our willingness to share their sorrow, and we left to God the healing that only He can give. But we gave something else too—our hope. The night after Cameron's funeral, John said with a knowing smile (as only he could), "Well, now I have a friend in heaven."

"Yes, John," we agreed. "We all do."

# 28

# Crowning Glory

John was feeling the love at Chaminade. His classmates called out to him as he passed them in the hall, led by his faithful aide, Cody. It was frustrating to John that they would rarely identify themselves, assuming that he had the capacity to recognize their many unique voices. But he heard their genuine affection, and that's what mattered most.

Understandably, teachers were initially apprehensive about having John in their classes. After all, they took jobs at Chaminade with the expectation that they would be teaching high-functioning kids with bright futures. But John slowly began to win them over. In time, they began requesting to have John in their classes and helping him to maximize his opportunities. As a result, he was able to do some amazing things for someone with his limitations. He helped to build and to control robots in science competitions, for example, and he tried his hand at sculpture.

He even joined the track team during his junior year. I went to the practices with him, and hand in hand we ran around the track. We weren't setting any records. His stride had shortened as his muscles had begun to contract. He didn't move with the same grace he had when he was younger. But he strained and pushed and worked up a sweat. He knew he couldn't compete with the others, but that knowledge didn't bother him much. He wanted only to be engaged with his peers as much as he could. If heart alone could win races, he would have been the state champ.

One day, as the rest of the team was off running fast somewhere and we were slowly plodding around the track, John slumped over in a seizure. I pulled him onto the football field and held him until the seizure was over. No one else witnessed the incident. Strangely, it felt like a private event in a very public place. A custodian saw me carrying John back to the locker room and offered to help. I turned down the offer. Something inside me wanted to carry my son alone. After about a hundred yards I started to feel stupid. John was getting heavy. Although I had already learned a hundred times before that God did not intend for me to carry my burdens alone, that stubborn ego of mine needed another lesson.

John never was a track star, but by living courageously he became royalty. In the fall of his senior year, Brother Tom, the principal, asked Lori and me to attend the homecoming rally. "John has been nominated to the homecoming court," he said.

At the rally, Lori and I sat in the bleachers and watched the happy youthful couples promenade to the middle of the gym to their favorite songs. The kids all looked so cool. They danced, waved, and joked as they moved. The air was electric.

The intensity dramatically increased when the names of John and his date, a beauty queen who had participated in various pageants, were called. Over the loudspeaker came "Take Me Out to the Ball Game", and the kids cheered wildly for them. But as they made their way down a short set of stairs, Lori and I held our breaths. We were pretty sure that the beauty queen wouldn't look so good if John tripped and pulled her down with him. Luckily, she was able to guide John with great grace, and we were all spared any disasters.

As the smiling couple basked in everyone's admiration, the moment seemed perfect. But God does not stop at what we think is enough. If we but open our hands to receive whatever He wills to give us, He pours out His gifts and blessings in exuberant abundance. And so John and his date were declared homecoming king and queen, and the cheering and shouting for joy nearly blew off the roof. I couldn't see because the tears were pouring down my face. And I wasn't the only one. Lori was wiping her eyes on my shirt.

# 29

# Ben Tackles High School

When Ben entered high school in 2009, we longed for him to have the same enriching experiences his brother was having at Chaminade, but Ben had his own ideas about what he wanted to do. And he approached high school the way he approached everything else—at full speed.

In spite of Batten's, our sons were very like other brothers. As the firstborn steps naturally into his glorious place in the universe, the second son drives harder and faster to keep up with his big brother.

Ben's temperament was completely different from his older brother's. John had the capacity to sit still and listen; Ben did not. If John didn't understand what was being discussed in class (which was probably most of the time), he faked it and at least appeared attentive. Ben just dropped his head on the desk and began snoring loudly.

Ben carved his own path, and he benefited from every possible tax dollar spent by the public school system at Agoura High. He signed up for cooking class, physical education (twice a day), wood shop, and a couple of classes that at least sounded as though they could entail some mental effort, even though cognitively he couldn't work anywhere near grade level. He threw himself into everything he did as if heedless of his limitations. He didn't even seem to notice that he was mostly blind.

The school tried to put Ben into some mainstream classes with modified work, but in most of these he became frustrated and distracted. The few exceptions were physical education and art. He couldn't see much, but he didn't lack artistic vision.

After getting a class schedule that made me envious, Ben signed up for the wrestling team. The coach thought he could learn to wrestle despite his visual impairment. After practicing with the team for a couple of weeks, Ben realized that he couldn't stand the smell of thirty sweaty teenage bodies confined to a room about the size of a closet. Lori, for one, was thrilled when Ben decided to give up the sport. Apparently, the smell did not appeal to her either.

For the most part, Ben thrived at Agoura, thanks to the adaptations the school made on his behalf. He probably stressed out a few teachers to the point of early retirement, because he could be a handful. Some days he would have what came to be known as "Cameron meltdowns", when his anxiety, pain, frustration, or grief overwhelmed his capacity to cope. He would fall apart and wail over all his losses at once.

"Why did Cameron kill himself?"

"Why can't I drive?"

"Why can't John see?" (To this day he never asks that question about himself.)

Why and why and why?

No one could give him acceptable answers. Perhaps there are none. All most of us could do was let the episode run its course and keep assuring him of our love.

At 6-foot-3 and far north of 240 pounds, his aide, Harvey, was a blessing. An ex-navy guy, Harvey had the emotional and physical toughness to hold Ben back when necessary and the sensitivity to allow Ben to cry it all out when his little body couldn't keep it all in. He adopted and loved Ben as his own son. He traveled the highs and the lows with him—an incredible feat for anyone else, but nothing unusual for Saint Harvey the Large.

Despite his many challenges, Ben had a must-do, not a can-do, spirit. He wanted to drive (and sometimes I let him), and during his junior year he pleaded to join the football team. Coach Wegher yielded to Ben and gave him a uniform and some pads, but despite Ben's stout heart, the coach could not let him play. Ben gave the coach a good deal of abuse over this line in the sand, and he handled it with much grace (the coach, that is, not Ben). Ben argued with anyone who would listen, stomped, and even shed some tears, but he was not going to play football. Some obstacles simply can't be overcome—a tough lesson for anyone to learn.

On game nights, Ben and I paced the sidelines. As the plays were called over the loudspeakers and the excited fans cheered, Ben screamed to be put into the game. He was willing to throw himself blindly (literally) against the opponent. Then he would ask, "Are they cheering for me too, Dad?"

"The whole team, Ben. And you are on the team."

"One play, Dad. Can't I just hold on to someone's arm? I can run. I want to feel what it's like to be tackled. If I get hurt, I won't ask again."

Eventually Ben learned to make the most of standing on the sidelines. He cheered like nobody's business. Of course, 99 percent of the time he had no idea what was going on. He knew only that someone always had to be tackled. Having memorized some of the players' names, he would call out to them to take care of business, even if they weren't on the field.

Finally, Ben found peace when he understood that love was the thing preventing him from playing football.

"You mean the coach loves me and doesn't want me to get hurt? That's why I can't play?"

"Yes, Ben."

"You mean all my friends love me so much and don't want to see me get hurt?"

"Right."

"You mean all the kids love me, and they don't want to see me get crushed?"

"Yup."

"You mean—"

"That's right, Ben, they love you."

"Oh. But I'm still a part of the team, right?"

This conversation repeated itself many times, and the disappointment gradually subsided. Love soothed the wound the way only love can.

# 30

# On a Mission from God

As the other teens around us grew in knowledge, John and Ben faltered, and simple tasks such as tying shoes became difficult. As other kids ran track with blistering speed, our boys found walking increasingly laborious. As their peers developed active social lives, John and Ben spent more and more time at home. My boys continued to stay in the flow of life, but each day their boats moved a little slower.

John and Ben mostly accepted their limitations because they were loved and knew that love was the most beautiful thing in their lives. But they also knew that their illness locked them out of the normal activities and friendships that were being enjoyed by their peers, and the knowledge of their isolation sometimes brought the pain of loneliness.

As Lori and I pondered their situation, we grew in our understanding of what life is really all about: we are on a mission from God. God creates us, loves us, and sees us in ways that we and the rest of the world often miss. Of course, God sees our imperfections. Yet He also sees the glorious beings He intended from the beginning—the men and women He sacrificed for in order to bring them into eternal friendship with Him.

While striving to accept the limitations of our earthly lives, we Christians continually need to aspire to become the friends of God we are meant to be. A paradox, I know, but the God who made us is an artist, and we are His masterpieces in the making. As we look at the natural beauty of this planet, we see majesty. In the tiniest atom and in the largest star we are given a glimpse of the splendor of God. We too are His creatures, and we too are to glorify Him with all that He has given us.

God does not give everyone the same abilities, but He gives abilities to everyone. We gain nothing by coveting what other people have, but we gain heaven itself by using every gift God gives us to its fullest potential in order to glorify Him. The good news is that we do not have to rely only on ourselves to fulfill our potential. Rather, we can give everything we have been given back to the Father through the Son and let the transformative power of the Holy Spirit carry us along to where we need to be.

The most important gift that Lori and I could give our boys was the belief that they were specially and wonderfully made by the Artist of all artists, and that He calls them by name to be His friends. We needed to cling to this belief ourselves—that no matter the progression of the disease, no matter the hardships, our sons were beautiful creations of God, here on earth for a unique purpose that only they could fulfill.

In 2008 we were given an opportunity to speak about our challenges and blessings when a young friend of ours, Megan McEveety, asked to do a video about the boys as part of her senior project in film school. In the video, she captured a slice of our life. She showed the boys overcoming their handicaps: skiing, playing ball, and so forth, but she also showed the tears from dreams yet to be realized.

"If you could do anything, John," I asked, "what would it be?"

Quietly, with faltering speech and a shy smile, he replied, "Play baseball on my own team for my school."

An impossible dream. A prayer.

Two years later, time was running out: John was a senior, and he lacked the abilities needed to play baseball. It just so happened, however, that the varsity baseball coach, Frank Mutz, was on John's senior retreat and learned about his passion for baseball. He offered John the chance to suit up with the team and to join them in the dugout for every home game. And it didn't stop there. John was named the honorary captain of the team.

We all went to the games, and Cody, John's aide, or I would sit with John in the dugout. I would narrate the game—the hits, the pitches, the stolen bases. John would cheer, laugh, and smile. In the midst of several games, John suffered seizures during exciting moments. I would carry him away from the action, but when he awoke, he would want to be brought back to the dugout.

For John to letter in the sport, he needed to play in at least one game. During the final home game, there would be a lot on the line. Chaminade would face Alemany in a Mission League championship game. Yet Coach Mutz decided to play John, and he talked things over with the Alemany coach.

"Look, I got this kid on my team," Coach Mutz began. "We're gonna just take the out, but John's batting first, our designated hitter."

"Nope," Coach Thompson said. "You take an out, we take an out." In that moment, winning became about something more than scoring runs.

In true baseball fashion, both coaches probably spit some chew on the ground, scraped some dirt from their cleats, and maybe even scratched something or other. A real pitch would be too dangerous, both coaches agreed. John wouldn't be able to duck something he couldn't see. So John would swing at a ball on a stationary support, as in T-ball.

On May 12, 2010, John and I arrived at the field early. I led him into the batting cage and set up the tee for a little pregame warm-up. I was nervous. It's still hard to hit a ball on a tee if you can't see the tee. But John was all smiles.

Bill Plaschke of the *Los Angeles Times* showed up for the game. He had been tipped off by the principal of Saint Jude's, John's Catholic elementary school, who was working for Chaminade at the time. Plaschke was one of the biggest sports writers in the world. He didn't make me or John worry, though. We had no idea who he was.

When the time came for John to bat, we heard the announcement: "Now batting, number fifteen, John Sikorra."

Arm in arm, we stepped up to the plate, and I set up the tee. I placed John's hand on the ball so he could feel its location. Then I stepped a couple of feet away. "Swing away, buddy. Have fun. Do your best."

Both teams lined up outside the dugout. And then, *crack!* John crushed it. The ball flew right up the third-base line.

Coach Mutz told me to take first, but John and I had no intention of stopping. His hit wasn't going to be a sacrifice bunt. John had made enough sacrifices. This one cut was the answer to a thousand prayers.

I grabbed John's hand and said, "Run! Run! Don't stop!" And we didn't. We rounded the bases to cheers from both teams and the entire crowd in the stands. Then the Chaminade team rushed home plate and embraced and celebrated their captain.

"It was the most important at-bat I'd ever seen," Plaschke later said.

As Lori tucked John into bed that night, he asked over and over, "How far did I hit it? How far did I run?" Then he slipped into a peaceful sleep with a smile on his face.

The following day, John was on the front page of the *Los Angeles Times* sports section. But he didn't need the article read to him. He had lived it.

John graduated a couple of months later amidst wild cheers and thunderous applause. He didn't really get it completely. He couldn't see the crowd on their feet, he couldn't see the tears in their eyes, but I'm certain that his heart felt their love.

Chaminade was no more equipped to handle our special-needs son than any other school. But in the words of Jim Adams, the president, the school didn't allow fear to rule the decision to accept him. None of us knew how things would work, but we all set aside our fears and trusted. And the result was a taste of normal American high school life, with its dances and games and friendships, far beyond our wildest expectations.

The four years weren't a magic carpet ride. There were plenty of bumps along the way. But we had done our part, which was to allow ourselves to be loved. John's limitations proved to be not something to conquer or to be conquered by, but an invitation to John and to everyone around him to greatness of heart. We were blessed by all the people who chose to love John and to make accommodations for him. But I believe, if you asked them, that they would say *they* were the blessed ones.

# 31

# Big Changes

Just as time moves on, so must we. Our Chaminade experiences had been great, but they had to come to an end. New challenges were in store for our family.

Before graduation, Lori and I took Jim, the president of the school, Brother Tom, the principal, and John to lunch. We were sitting in a casual (affordable) but nice restaurant in Calabasas and feeling a bit melancholic because our time together was drawing to a close. The sadness subsided a bit when Jim looked at John and asked if he would consider coming back the following school year as a paid employee, as a kind of ambassador. He could come to Chaminade a couple of days a week and greet the kids, talk to them at lunchtime, that sort of thing.

Lori and I were so excited. "We can remain!" we inwardly cheered.

But without hesitation John said, "No. I will have graduated."

We were all silent. Then Jim added, "John, this would be a paid job. I don't think I've ever been turned down. Chaminade is number one—"

"No, thank you."

More silence.

Why was John the only one at the table who could let go? Perhaps he understood something we did not. Perhaps his failing memory was a gift: he could neither hold on to what had been nor anticipate what lay ahead. Perhaps he intuited the decline that was coming. Regardless, he just was, in the present moment.

Soon after graduation, John began needing more help with ordinary tasks. He was very good-natured about his increasing dependency. The resistance came from Mom and Dad, not because we weren't willing to help him, but because each new phase of the disease served as a stark reminder that it was progressing and his life was being cut short. We were constantly challenged by trying to find the right balance between living in the present and anticipating the future. There was little comfort (if any) in contemplating the past.

At the turn of the year, John began having seizures about once every seven to ten days. In February he got an upper respiratory infection, and his fever spiked to 105. Having learned from experience that whenever his immune system was weakened, he was even more prone to seizures, we decided to take him to the hospital to get ahead of the curve. He was given antibiotics and sent home, and by the next morning the fever was gone.

The next day, I drove Ben to school with John in the front passenger seat. As we got onto the freeway, John began to seize. Ben sprang into action, his stout heart leading him into the fray. He held John, keeping him safe, while I pulled over to the side of the freeway. There we waited for the seizure to end.

Later, when I brought John to the pediatrician, Ben came along. On the way, Ben started to feel sick. Lori met us at the doctor's office, and while there, Ben started to have dry heaves, John started to seize, and the doctor went for sedatives. (They were for him, I'm sure.) The little office took on the look of a three-ring circus. Calm returned, momentarily, and Lori and I took the boys home.

Around 7 P.M. John had another seizure, aspirated, and turned purple. Unfortunately, Lori was at home alone with the boys, as I was still at work. As Lori called the paramedics, Ben came downstairs and threw up. The paramedics arrived, took everyone's temperature (and whatever else), and after consulting with the doctor, helped the boys get back into bed.

"Let's watch and see," they all decided.

When I got home a couple of hours later, we decided I should stay with John to keep an eye on him.

John seemed agitated. We called the paramedics again, and when they arrived, John had another seizure, his fourth in a matter of hours. The paramedics sedated him and took him to the medical center at UCLA.

John didn't stop seizing until 6 A.M. the following morning. The emergency room doctor had said earlier that they might have to induce a coma, insert a tracheal tube, and put him on a respirator. Lori thought he was going to die and was visibly frightened. I showed little emotion. Later, Lori and I tried to reconcile how we could have the same experience yet respond so differently emotionally. I simply believed that John would be fine, I said. Was I in denial? Was I, as a man, more able to detach myself? Was I being spiritually consoled? I'm not sure. But as a nurse, Lori understood better than I did the severity of John's situation. And as a mother, she was feeling on a deep level everything that was happening to him.

Our different reactions caused us to feel somewhat distant from each other, a phenomenon that has been reported by other couples with seriously sick children. It has been said that the union of marriage provides stability in that when one is weak, the other can be strong. Sometimes, however, the union provides stability when tears or laughter are shared simultaneously.

Less than a week later, the seizures resumed, and John returned to the medical center. The doctors changed his medications, and the seizures stopped. In the meantime, the doctors discovered that John's heart rate was very slow, sometimes dropping into the twenties while he was sleeping. Looking into the problem, they discovered that a slow heartbeat can be another complication of Batten disease.

As Batten disease is so rare, few doctors know anything about it. So far, we had encountered only one doctor in Los Angeles who had ever treated a Batten's child. When other doctors met the boys, they dusted off their medical books and did their homework, and the best of them humbled themselves and called Dr. Jonathan Mink at the University of Rochester Medical Center. He is currently the nation's medical expert on Batten disease. The real experts, however, are the parents.

"I need to contact some of the parents," Lori said. She recalled hearing about Batten kids with pacemakers. Talking to their parents was difficult, however, because some of these children had died. One mother, God bless her, had three children with Batten's, and two of them had pacemakers inserted at a very advanced stage of the disease. They were alive, but just barely. She told Lori that the pacemakers had definitely lengthened her children's lives.

Knowing that our boys would die prematurely, Lori and I had already decided that we would aim for maximizing their quality of life not their quantity of years. We were open to inserting a pacemaker, so long as it would add to John's quality of life without causing him more suffering or prolonging his suffering. In other words, the benefits of the pacemaker would need to outweigh any burden it might cause him. One doctor warned that a pacemaker could theoretically keep John alive in a so-called vegetative state—not really the goal we were after. But the pediatric heart specialist thought it could give John more energy, which would make living easier for him.

It was difficult for Lori and me to know exactly what John was going through. He never complained about feeling bad, maybe because he didn't know anything else. We nevertheless concluded that we should have the pacemaker put in, and if it didn't make John feel better or give him more energy, we could just turn it off. While this course of action seemed to be the most reasonable, choosing it was one of the most difficult decisions we had ever made.

John couldn't grasp the concept of a pacemaker at all. So we used his favorite movie series to help him understand.

"You know, John, how Luke Skywalker sometimes has new parts put in, like when he gets his hand lopped off—"

Wait, that image wasn't going to bring him much comfort.

"You know how Darth Vader—"

No. Wrong character completely. John could never identify with evil.

"The pacemaker is like a Jedi power pack."

A smile spread across his face.

John recovered from the surgery without incident, and over the next couple of days, we started taking him for slow walks. He did fine, no complaints. But we didn't really notice any improvement in his energy level.

Then Alison took John for a walk. Hand in hand, just as on that first Halloween, they went off down the street.

"Man! He was dragging me along. I could hardly keep up!" Alison told us later.

Love and touch gave what technology alone couldn't.

Later that night, we said prayers with John. As he lay in bed quietly, his eyes filled with tears, which slowly rolled down his face. Then tears filled our eyes as well.

"What is it, John? Are you afraid?"

He shook his head.

John already had difficulty speaking in complete sentences, and being choked up didn't help.

We knew the hospital visit had confused and scared him. We spoke reassuringly.

"Travis," he finally got out.

"Travis your cousin?"

Again no.

"Heidi's son?"

Heidi was Lori's friend who had died of cancer a few years earlier. Travis was her son.

"Is *he* okay?" John managed.

"Travis is with his dad and brothers. He's loved. He's alive and well."

Death was again the topic of conversation in our home, and it spread a fog around Lori and me that temporarily prevented us from seeing the beauty of what lay ahead. And so we cried.

John too was crying—not for the mother who had died, but for those who remained. What was it that he saw that we could not?

# 32

# Warrior Angel

Aptly, when Ben spoke about heaven, he said he wanted to be a warrior angel and carry a giant sword. (Look out, demons! There's a new sheriff in town!) Ben's energy sometimes made it a little difficult to see his goodness, his holiness, yet his hunger and thirst for righteousness put him in the camp of the blessed.

If Ben had lived in Jesus' time, he would have been a combination of John the Baptist, living in the desert, and Peter, the first to go for the sword when trouble arose. Ben knew how to step up and meet challenges head-on.

When he was taking classes at the local church in preparation for his Confirmation, he was required to attend a weekend retreat with about a hundred other teenagers. In spite of his usual impetuousness, he was reluctant to go. He rarely spent time away from home, for obvious reasons. Knowing that he would be dependent on others to find the bathroom and to eat his meals made him anxious. But when he learned that he could bring a parent, he decided to go for it, and Lori "volunteered" me for the job.

Some parents opposed Ben's participation in the retreat. They thought he might distract the other kids and rob them of their experience. As I saw it, kids could learn about living holy lives and discuss the value of attending to the needs of the less fortunate, or they could live with someone less fortunate and grow in the virtue of charity by putting it into practice. The woman who ran the program, Denise Cortez, saw the opportunity for growth as I did and insisted that Ben attend the retreat.

The weekend retreat took place at a monastery in the high desert mountains of San Bernardino. The grounds were suited to handle large groups, with plenty of room for rowdy kids to lose themselves in the outdoors if they couldn't quite lose themselves in prayer. There were separate dormitories for the boys and girls (and plenty of chaperones to ensure they remained that way), and several small apartments. The chapel was modern, with stadium-style seating that circled the altar.

I initially thought that part of my job was to contain Ben. In some respects, it was, but Ben's larger-than-life attitude was not easily contained. Like a mighty river, it couldn't be stopped, though there were some chances of redirecting it.

At one of the first evening meals, Denise asked if one of the kids would like to pray the blessing. Ben's hand shot up first and definitely with the most enthusiasm. I cringed, just a little. I hoped that Ben would do the traditional prayer before meals so that everyone could join in. Right. I'll-Do-It-My-Way Ben went the extemporaneous route. "Ah ... Bless the Passion, holy, bless, Jesus, and the holiness, and Hail Mary, um, Our Father, who aren't, ah, and the Passion, and the food, and the ... Amen!" Straight from Ben's heart to the throne of God. Surely He heard the beauty and the praise.

Without missing a beat, a chorus of voices rang out, "Amen!"

Denise ran a powerful retreat and made fantastic use of the teen leaders. In the chapel, the kids gathered around a large cross wrapped in foil. Then, on a small piece of paper they wrote down a sin they thought was keeping them from having a closer relationship with God. I helped Ben to write down his sin. Then the kids pinned their papers to the cross and asked for God's forgiveness. The cross was lit, and in a flash the sins burned up.

One paper remained, however. One of the other retreat leaders tried to light it again. Then again. He held the flame to the paper, but it refused to burn. I looked closer and saw it was Ben's. Yielding to the stubborn paper, the leader removed it from the cross and discreetly put it in his pocket.

What did all that mean? I can't say for sure, but God seemed to be saying that He accepted Ben as he was, that He saw the beautiful soul hidden behind his infirmities. Ben and I both knew that to a certain degree, despite Batten disease, he was capable of sin, that is, of deliberately refusing to do what he knew was right. But because of the disease, so much of Ben's defiant behavior was the result of a brokenness over which he had no control. God alone knows us completely, I was being reminded.

God has paid the price for the times we have turned away from Him. So we can give Him our sins and let Him take them away. And then they are gone. God no longer sees them.

Later, the kids participated in the Hall of Oppression. In small groups, they were led blindfolded (Ben played along) into a dormitory, where the blindfolds were removed. They then entered a number of rooms that were dimly lit with an eerie reddish glow.

In the first room, a teenager sat on the edge of a bed. A gun lay next to him. He was crying as he wrote a pain-filled good-bye letter to his parents. His voice cracked as he described feeling very alone. Suddenly, he set down the pen, picked up the gun, and put it to his head. The lights went out as he fell backward.

In the bathroom, girls were throwing up in toilets surrounded by posters of perfect bodies. Written on the pictures were the words "I'm fat" or "I'm ugly."

Bullies greeted us in another room. We were forced to wear signs with the words "Nigger", "Fag", "Wetback", and "Gimp" and to endure their insults. As we experienced being targets of hatred, we got a taste of being "the other". Finally, Ben could take it no more. First, in a small voice, he said, "Shut up." Then his protests grew bigger and bigger. He was ready to fight. He couldn't see the aggressors, but he was ready to take them on and take his chances. I led him out of the building. He had experienced enough.

It was past midnight when the last of the retreatants had visited all the rooms. Afterward, all the kids went to the chapel to process their feelings. Everyone was exhausted. Resistance was low. One teenage boy began to cry.

"I go to school with Ben," the young man said. "I've seen kids tease him. Ben doesn't know."

Soon they all were crying. They knew they had wronged Ben either by teasing him or by remaining silent as someone else teased him. As Edmund Burke said, "The only thing necessary for the triumph of evil is for good men to do nothing." And it was Ben's outspoken outrage at the injustice he heard in the Hall of Oppression that awakened everyone else to this truth.

Throughout the weekend, the teens wrote letters of affirmation to each other. A girl offered to read Ben's letters to him—one letter after another.

Ben started to cry. "I didn't know so many kids love me." It's quite possible that many of those kids didn't know they loved Ben either, until they retreated from their ordinary surroundings, took an honest look at their behavior, and allowed themselves to be challenged to do better.

The next day, the kids were asked to write letters to their parents, telling them one thing they may not know. The leader helped Ben to write his.

"Ben, do you want to tell your parents how much you love them?"

"No. They already know that."

"What would you like them to know, Ben?"

"That even though it's been a long time, I still miss Cameron. I cry a lot."

# 33

# Ben and Mary, Again

When Lori and I realized that Ben was still grieving Cameron's death, we had to accept the fact that there was little, if anything, we could do about it. One of the hardest lessons for parents to learn is that they can't give their children everything they need. Sometimes the thing a child needs can come only from the realm above, the place Buzz Lightyear calls "infinity and beyond".

At every step along the way, Lori and I tried to give John and Ben the words that would comfort them as they struggled against Batten disease. John led the way in the fight against death and despair. That was his burden. But in some ways, Ben carried an even greater weight: he witnessed his brother's decline with just enough foresight to see what lay ahead for *him*. Perhaps the sense of his own doom was one of the reasons Cameron's suicide haunted him. Regardless, Lori and I could see that our encouraging words were not enough for Ben. He needed heavenly consolation.

Early one morning, Ben came into our bedroom. He was seventeen at the time but psychologically much younger. He looked shaken and scared. He climbed into bed and said, "Mary came into my room last night. Cameron was with her."

He went on to describe what he saw, which, in itself, was interesting, as Ben can't see.

"Cameron was dressed in black clothes. Mary had dark brown eyes and a grey robe. She had the most beautiful flowers I've ever seen and a gold crown on her head."

Cameron then said to Mary, "Mom, Ben is scared. We need to go. Let's go, Mother, let's go."

Mary looked at Ben and said, "He's with me, Ben. He's okay. He's all right."

Ben then said that Mary "flew out" of his room and "went back up into heaven." He added, "I don't want her to come back, though. I was afraid."

Days later, when Lori was lying with Ben in his bed, he insisted that she look out the window and up into the sky.

"Up there, Mom. Look out my window and you can see heaven." He pointed. "Right there. Look, Mom. That's where heaven is. That's where Mary and Cameron flew to." He enthusiastically described heaven as brilliant blue and yellow light. It was rich with other colors too.

Later Ben tried to talk further with Lori and me about heaven. But as it was difficult for him to articulate what he saw and experienced, we decided to drop the subject. For several nights afterward, however, he refused to sleep in his room. He was scared.

A couple of weeks later, Ben made another early-morning visit to our bed.

"Mary came into my room again last night. She looked into my eyes."

Some might ask why Mary, and not the Lord Himself, was so present to Ben. I don't know. In our home we talk a lot about Jesus and the eternal life with Him that is yet to come. But maybe Ben needed to hear the loving voice of a mother.

Lori noted that Ben was no longer grieving for Cameron the way he had been before. Mary, she said, seemed to have consoled Ben in a way that she, his earthly mother, could not. Human wisdom, apparently, even from the lips of a loving mother, couldn't compete with what heaven had offered him.

A couple of weeks later, Ben came to our bedroom with another early-morning update.

"Mary came again," he said calmly. "Why don't her feet ever touch the ground?"

Ben kept grabbing Lori's hand and holding it in different ways. It started to bug her, and she asked Ben to stop.

But Ben grabbed her hand again and said, "This is how she held my hand."

"Who, Ben?"

"Mary. Then she told me, 'Don't be afraid, Ben. I'm with you.'"

That's the message of the Gospels. Over and over Jesus said, "Don't be afraid. I am with you."

That night, Ben went to sleep, unafraid, even though he was sure he would be visited again by Mary. The next morning, at Mass, Ben sat quietly in the pew, grabbing his own hand as though someone else were holding it.

# 34

# Alison and Lily

If his life had been different, if John had been blessed with good health, it would have been our wish, and John's too, no doubt, that he marry Alison. Ever since that first Halloween together, they loved each other.

Because of John's illness, his love for Alison, and hers for him, never could have been fulfilled in the marital embrace. Yet the two of them witnessed the kind of love that results when grace builds on nature.

Ten years after Alison and John first trick-or-treated together, Lori and I needed some help with the boys, and Alison stepped up. The support she gave became a part-time job for her, but she became a full-time part of our lives.

John was clearly smitten. Their hands touching and their gentle words to each other made his face shine more than anything Lori and I did for him at the time. I guess the shift was the inevitable replacement all parents eventually have to face.

Alison would take John on walks. It didn't matter where they went, for he couldn't go far. The content of their conversation wasn't important, since by then his words were sparse and sometimes difficult to understand. He communicated all he needed with his beautiful smile, and she communicated all she needed with her gentle touch.

I have learned through my studies, my work, and my experience that we live longer, survive calamities better, and experience more joy when we develop our relationships and see them, not our material blessings, as the most important treasures in our lives. Human interconnectedness is important because it helps us to get outside of ourselves and reach out to others. And we really are happiest when we are doing things for others.

Studies, clinical practice, and my own experience show that even connections between humans and animals help people to thrive. For example, the other morning I came downstairs early, poured my coffee, and saw my faithful (and hungry) dog sitting ever so cutely. I imagined that she was looking at me with love in her eyes. (I can't really manage love in my eyes until after my first cup of coffee.)

"Lily," I said, "would you like breakfast?"

She wagged her tail. Oh, how she adores me.

"Would you like steak and eggs, fluffy pancakes, or this crunchy crap in the giant red bag?"

The tail really went to town!

"Crunchy crap or steak? Which one?"

Oh, she was so excited!

Then, as though my next line were going to be even funnier if I said it loudly: "CRUNCHY CRAP? YOU GOT IT! HERE YOU GO, LILY!"

For a minute, we connected. We made eye contact. I took care of the needs of another living creature, and I felt good doing it. My morning became a little brighter.

## 35

# Ben Gets a Job

During the summer before his senior year of high school, Ben spent considerable energy in pursuit of a job. Quite entrepreneurial, he took a stab at being a door-to-door salesman by peddling lemons from our tree to the neighbors. He heard his friends talk about going off to college, and he wasn't about to be left out.

"I need money to buy books and a new computer," he told Lori and me. Actually, he told everybody, even people he didn't know.

We weren't about to remind him of the obvious, that he couldn't read or use a computer. We just loved the fact that he was excited about assuming responsibility for his education and development. I had never heard of a kid so enthusiastic about buying his own school books.

Ben waited impatiently as a new Chick-fil-A was being built in our community. As soon as they started accepting job applications, Lori stopped in and spoke with the owner.

"My son, Ben, has always wanted a job. And we really love Chick-fil-A," Lori said.

"Here's an application."

"I don't think ... He can't fill it out. He can't write. He can't see. But he's a *great* kid. And I think he would work for free food."

A moment of silence. Then, "I'd like to meet him."

The next day, I brought Ben to the restaurant to meet the owner.

"So, Ben, what do you like to do?"

"I help these kids at my school who can't see good and have problems. I sit with them ..."

It took only a couple of minutes for Joseph, the owner, to see Ben's heart and courage.

"I'd love for you to work here, Ben."

Ben started to hyperventilate. Tears filled his eyes.

"Oh my gosh! I can give everyone free food, and—"

"No, Ben. We can't give the food away, but *you* can eat it."

Deal!

Ben never considered that he might have difficulty doing what would be asked of him. He simply basked in the joy of being wanted. And he never asked about the pay. He was no longer focused on buying books. For him the job was about something other than money. Something better.

The owner, however, assured Ben (and me) that he would indeed pay him for his hours. My side of the bargain was to promise that Lori or I would accompany Ben during his two-hour shift each Saturday.

Ben and I showed up about a half hour early for his first day on the job (clearly inspired by the idea of free food). Ben was assigned to accompany the Chick-fil-A cow and wave to people as they drove by in their cars. He tried his best to keep the company secret that it wasn't a real dancing cow but a young man in a costume. Still, he conspiratorially confided this fact to a few adult patrons.

There was a lot of learning to do, for Lori and me as much as for Ben. After each shift, Lori or I would brag about the new skill mastered that day.

"I washed dishes today," Lori said one Saturday.

"What? How many things of soap do you use? I haven't done that yet."

She seemed to beat me to all the firsts. She squeezed lemons for the lemonade, she filled condiments, she helped Ben call out names when food was ready to be picked up. I think I was better only at emptying the garbage.

Sometimes during my shift with Ben, I would daydream (don't tell the boss) and wonder, "Why did I get my master's degree in psychology? Why did I spend those years learning about relationships?"

"Oh yeah," I would remind myself, "the relationship in front of me—that's what matters. Put your learning into practice and be present to Ben."

After Ben's first day at Chick-fil-A, while the family was still celebrating, an old friend of mine called. We began exchanging pleasantries and describing our kids' recent accomplishments.

"Ben is an assistant to the dancing cow at Chick-fil-A," I began.

Kent then spoke about his daughter, who had just graduated from Officer Candidate School at the Marine Corps base in Quantico, Virginia, where she was the honor graduate out of a class of 535. She won the Daughters of the American Revolution award and the physical fitness award, scoring 100 percent for combat fitness, including on the obstacle course (setting a Marine Corps record for women). She was entering her senior year at the University of Southern California and would be studying abroad in Scotland. She was a beautiful person physically, spiritually, and emotionally.

Finally Kent paused and said, "Joe, I don't mean to brag. I know you have your struggles, and I know you are proud of your kids."

"Kent, you should be proud of your daughter. And I am just as proud of Ben."

I meant what I said. Kent's daughter's accomplishments in no way diminished those of Ben. God gives everyone a unique set of talents and abilities. We are not to compare ourselves, or our children, with others but are to be grateful for whatever God, in His wisdom, gives us and to use it as well as we can to serve Him. Perhaps this truth is a bit easier to grasp when the high point of one's day is taking out the garbage at Chic-fil-A so that a child can stand beside a guy in a cow costume.

# 36

# Defying Gravity

On August 18, 2012, we celebrated John's twenty-first birthday. When our family was first given the Batten diagnosis, we weren't sure John would live long enough to see that day, never mind be able to celebrate it.

Thanks to the generosity of a special friend, we took the family to Disneyland, along with John's friend Andy, whom he had met in first grade, and Alison, our current helper and the love of John's life. Though we spoke little of it, Lori and I both nursed a little anxiety about the day.

John had slowed down considerably over the previous year, and we knew there was no way his legs would support all the walking at the park. Making the decision to use a wheelchair seemed like an admission that the disease was gaining traction, but in truth, we didn't have a choice. Gravity was doing its best to take him—and us—down.

The Disney guide showed up with the wheelchair, John dropped in, and off we went, moving through the park with ease. Getting on and off the rides wasn't easy, but the shared laughter and excitement quickly erased the unease we felt about the wheelchair. Our anxiety, our fear, served us how? Not at all.

After sundown, we watched the laser light show in the California Adventure part of the theme park. The show, using water cannons, lasers, and colorful animation, is a spectacular visual feast. But what could that all mean to a young man who can't see any of it? Days later, however, when we were talking about the memorable day, John kept saying the words "light show". Not Space Mountain or Mickey, but "light show".

At last we understood. The light show was set to the music of all the Disney cartoons and movies John had watched through the years: *The Lion King, Beauty and the Beast, Aladdin, Enchanted, Finding Nemo.* I don't believe the music brought him back to the sights he could remember but rather stirred his heart with the love he had felt his whole life.

That John was still alive at twenty-one and still capable of experiencing the joy that comes from knowing he is loved proved to me that our family had indeed defied gravity, at least for a time.

# 37

# Nearing the End, but Not Really

As we entered the summer of 2013, both our boys were more than simply staying alive. They were defying not only gravity but categorization.

At his high school graduation, Ben won an award for being "Best Senior Ever". Talk about overachievers. He was given a plaque with raised lettering and an image of a football player. He couldn't stop running his fingers over it throughout the ceremony. The image, his name in raised letters—the award meant so much to him. Unbelievably, Agoura High produced twenty-two valedictorians. Ben, however, got the only standing ovation on graduation day. The presenter spoke of Ben's goodness and heart. I can imagine no greater achievement. Truly, he had the heart of a lion.

Ben's high school years had been tough on all of us. In some ways, he was no different from any other trying teenager. He had the same testosterone and desires as other adolescent males, but he lacked some of the physical and mental abilities to channel them productively. By his senior year, however, he had mellowed out a bit. Whenever he found something funny, everyone around him was lifted by his exuberant laughter.

For his graduation present, he wanted to do some traveling. The first trip we made was back to Fontana Lake, where we had taken the boys after receiving John's diagnosis and where Ben had learned to wakeboard. Ben wanted to be with family. He wanted to play. So did I.

John did not want to go. "Too hard," he said. He now relished the comfort and the security of home.

"Come on, John," I urged. "The water." I wasn't ready to let go of an experience that had always been able to bring us together, even in the most difficult circumstances. Although we had been given a death sentence, we had found life in abundance at the ocean, at the lake, beside mountain streams. Water. It represented togetherness, joy, and above all, life. In experiencing God's creation of water, we had been able to embrace His gift of life and to see *Him*.

"John, the water ..."

My urging was going nowhere. John's adventures in the great outdoors had come to an end. He was at peace, lying with us on the couch, sitting on the porch swing, taking a spin in the "Dodgers Glide Ride" (his wheelchair). He didn't need what was out there. He needed only the grace that lived in his heart and in the love of those around him.

He didn't long for the water anymore. Not that water.

I made the trip alone with Ben. Lori stayed at home with John, tenderly caring for him. Their time together was simple and quiet. They shared meals, movies, prayers, and walks. The time was holy.

Ben and I played hard—really hard. And, not surprisingly, Ben found his way into the *Smokey Mountain Times*, the local newspaper. Everything he did seemed to draw attention. With his Uncle Danny, we white-water rafted, water-skied, wakeboarded, tubed behind the boat, zip-lined through the trees, and listened to the thunder roar through the mountains during evening storms.

In a whisper, Jesus' words flowed into me.

"The water, Joe."

"The water?"

"Water."

I knew He didn't mean the silky-smooth stuff I like to play in, but rather another kind of water.

Now when the Lord knew that the Pharisees had heard that Jesus was making and baptizing more disciples than John (although Jesus himself did not baptize, but only his disciples), he left Judea and departed again to Galilee. He had to pass through Samaria. So he came to a city of Samaria, called Sychar, near the field that Jacob gave to his son Joseph. Jacob's well was there, and so Jesus, wearied as he was with his journey, sat down beside the well. It was about the sixth hour.

There came a woman of Samaria to draw water. Jesus said to her, "Give me a drink." For his disciples had gone away into the city to buy food. The Samaritan woman said to him, "How is it that you, a Jew, ask a drink of me, a woman of Samaria?" For Jews have no dealings with Samaritans. Jesus answered her, "If you knew the gift of God, and who it is that is saying to you, 'Give me a drink,' you would have asked him and he would have given you living water." The woman said to him, "Sir, you have nothing to draw with, and the well is deep; where do you get that living water? Are you greater than our father Jacob, who gave us the well, and drank from it himself, and his sons, and his cattle?" Jesus said to her, "Every one who drinks of this water will thirst again, but whoever drinks of the water that I shall give him will never thirst; the water that I shall give him will become in him a spring of water welling up to eternal life." (Jn 4:1–14)

The wet stuff would always remain my place for rejuvenation, fun, and even meditation. Water equaled life. But God was reminding me of the everlasting water, the water

He alone can give. He was preparing me for the end that was approaching.

Later that summer, Lori took Ben to New Orleans to watch Ryan Griffin play his first preseason game as a New Orleans Saint. It seemed like yesterday when John stood alongside Ryan at Chaminade as his "water hydration specialist". That same weekend, Lori and Ben went with friends to take their daughter to college. A part of Lori was sad that she would never drop off her boys at college, let alone feel the pride of watching them play professional sports or accomplish other great feats. But she realized that this kind of comparing and competing wouldn't bring her joy. Rather, celebrating with those who were celebrating, sharing in their joy, is what made her trip a wonderful experience.

As the boys declined, I continued to be inspired by their spirit. Like my wife's trust twenty-five years earlier, when she sat on my shoulders as we raced across the lake, their courage made me want to be found worthy of them—and not just of them, but of the grace that had been so generously poured out for us.

The fact is, our sons were not supposed to have been so healthy for so long. Our family was not supposed to have been so happy. Our marriage was not supposed to have endured the strain of two special-needs children. We had broken all the records. We were alive and well in so many ways.

In some ways, I believe, our story is unique. Yet I also believe it is everyone's story. We will all experience illness and death. We will all face circumstances and losses that make us ask why. We will all be tested beyond what we think are our limits. And at the outermost edge of our limits, where our faith in God will be challenged to the utmost, we will be given the choice either to grow in the grace God offers us (and be taken to a place beyond our wildest imagination) or to shrink back in fear.

As John was nearing the finish line of his race on earth, often friends, and sometimes strangers, approached us and said, "I don't know how you do it, Joe and Lori. What a cross; what a burden. Yet we see you in church, in the community, and see love, patience, and tenderness."

The truth is, without the amazing power of God I could not have made the journey. I could never have relied on the power of Joe. Although I didn't always recognize it, God's grace sustained me, and it was often delivered through the many friends, relatives, and sometimes strangers (and angels) who helped us along the way.

Just before Christmas, John started to lose his appetite for food and drink, and by New Year's Lori and I knew he needed a feeding tube.

Other Batten's parents said the feeding tube was one of the more difficult decisions they made, but, once they made it, they wondered why they had struggled over it. Administering drugs and nourishment is so much easier with a feeding tube.

"So you are going all the way?" asked the boys' doctor when we requested a feeding tube.

There was no question. John might have been losing weight, but not the smile that could transform hearts—ours included.

# 38

# Lori

While we were wrestling with the decision over the feeding tube, Lori was wrestling with pain of her own. Her back was aching. An imaging test revealed a spot in her abdomen that led her to Dr. Richard Frieder.

Twenty-two years ago, at John's cesarean-section birth, Dr. Frieder gave me my first anatomy lesson. After he pulled John out of Lori's abdomen, he said, "See, Joe? These are Lori's ovaries. And here are the fallopian tubes."

"Doctor, her pressure is dropping."

"Oh. We better get this all back inside and close her up."

I watched in awe, but Lori never forgave the doctor and me.

In December 2013, Dr. Frieder told Lori she had a cyst on her ovary.

"I don't like the look of it," he said. "Come back in a few weeks." When Lori saw him again on January 20, he noticed that the cyst had grown—a lot.

Late that afternoon, she pulled her car into the driveway but didn't come in. At first I thought she had bumped into some neighbor's car (again) and was trying to buff away the evidence. After a little while, I went outside to find her. She was sitting on the swing with tears in her eyes. I sat down beside her.

"He thinks it might be cancer," she said. "He wants to take it out. He has a cancer specialist who will do the operation with him. If it's cancer, they'll want to start chemo right away."

A few days later life got *really* stressful. The little hospital Lori worked for refused to allow her health coverage to pay for surgery by her doctor at the hospital in Santa Monica.

"We can do it here," they said, "So, blah, blah, blah."

I told her we could sell the house. We'll pay for it. Maybe another doctor could do the procedure, but Lori's peace of mind was important too. She needed to be treated by the doctor she knew and trusted in spite of the anatomy lesson. Perhaps the doctor who had delivered our two boys could now deliver her from this nightmare.

The war was on. Angry calls were made. Though we had God on our side, we forgot that sometimes. But in spite of our weak moments, Lori's requests were granted.

We entered Saint John's Hospital. The morning light infused the four-story atrium. On the wall an inscription read, "The greatest of these is charity." Yes. Love. The conqueror of fear.

Dr. Frieder told me before the surgery, "If it's cancer, I'll come out and let you know right away while the cancer surgeon finishes up. If it's not, he'll come out and meet with you while I finish up."

Several stressful hours into the procedure, I got a phone call from a hospital line. What the heck? They didn't tell me what a call would mean. But I'll let Lori explain everything in her own words, in this edited version of something she later posted on her Facebook page:

> Today I turn fifty. For my gift this year, life gave me a rare opportunity to experience God's love in a unique way. Life threw out at me the scare of ovarian cancer. And then I won a total hysterectomy and an estrogen patch. Now

I know you are saying, "What the heck? Where's the gift in that?"

Well, one day after my doctor told me of his concerns, I received an e-mail from a complete stranger from my high school (from thirty years ago; I know, the Stone Age) stating that recently God had placed *me* on her heart to pray for. Of course, she was quite confused and completely unaware of my situation. Curiosity got to her and she contacted me though mutual friends. Quickly she understood my need for some serious prayers and joined in with my prayer warriors for a good outcome. Can you imagine getting an e-mail from someone you don't know, stating that God has asked her to pray for you? And then have that person actually do it, find you, and tell you that she is praying for you?

Then my sister Suzanne called to say she is coming for two weeks to help keep my house running while I recover. Then my sister Annie stated that she plans to be at the house as well each night during the weeks following my surgery. Who knew when we were younger and throwing shoes at each other that we would be each other's nursemaids? Biggest blessing.

My wonderful friend brought me my very own blanky prior to surgery and then continued to bless me with a gift each day prior to my big birthday. Meals were delivered before anyone had time to ask, "What's for dinner?" My friends of twenty-five years, our "supper club", drove three hours to celebrate an intimate, quiet, and peaceful dinner. I have received amazing cards, wonderful meals, and loving visits. My favorite cake ever, German chocolate, was delivered to my front door the night before my birthday. Overwhelming.

I was never afraid of cancer; why, so many people are diagnosed with cancer daily. I was concerned only for my dear husband and kids and how they would manage as I went through chemotherapy. And the thought of death didn't even scare me, only sadness for my son Ben. You see, my son John, I believe, already lives with the angels. He only hangs out with us to soothe us for a while longer. But Ben would have experienced too much sadness in one young person's life. And Joe, he has complete understanding that this life is just a blink and that the true sweetness lies ahead of us in heaven. Perhaps you're still asking where is the gift in all this?

Well, you see, God held his "doubting Thomas" by the hand, my hand, and once again showed me His unfailing love. Before I could even ask, He took care. Before I could gain strength to ask for prayer, He already had someone praying. Before I could ask for help in my home, the reservations were made. Before I even knew how much I would need a cozy blanky, it was delivered. And before I knew I would be ready to celebrate *no cancer*, the party was planned. God was always one step ahead of me.

We are so completely loved. If only I could just learn to be still, to be quiet, to calm my spirit and truly trust at the first moment of distress. Oh, how I am trying.

I love growing older. Well, maybe not all things, like bigger jeans, and gray hair, but what a blessing to buy bigger jeans and to color my hair, and hang around this world to see how else God will reveal His love. To my wonderful friends near and far, thank you for loving me, thank you for loving my family, and thank you for praying for us. Here's to fifty, and here's to my being married to a younger man for another six months.

I think about death and dying a lot, something that's only natural, given the situation my family is in. The surprise, perhaps, is that reflecting on death inspires me to live more fully, more adventurously, by seeing the opportunities and the blessings in everything that happens. I ask fewer why questions and say *why not* more frequently. And I desire more than ever to share the ups and downs of life with others, to encourage them by giving witness to the transformation through struggle and the healing through love that I observe in the people around me.

Life is short. Whether you are blessed with eighty years or eight, in the context of eternity, there isn't much difference. For the most part, we cannot control how much time we are given. But we are given a choice as to how we want to live: with the courage to embrace the adventure of living or with fear.

# 39

# A Knock at the Door

By the grace of God, my practice had begun to provide enough, coupled with Lori's part-time work as a nurse, for us to eke out a living. But no amount of hard work could ever achieve all the blessings God had provided throughout our journey. For the most part, trust had replaced fear. Funny, when we concentrate on the essentials (i.e., enough to eat, a roof above our heads, etc.) and on Him, God opens the storeroom of heaven and pours out blessings in astonishing ways.

A couple of years earlier I had written out a prayer, sealed it in an envelope, and, well, had forgotten about it. I'm pretty sure that's not what you're supposed to do with a prayer, but I'll comfort myself with the belief that God doesn't have such a feeble memory. Writing the prayer (not the forgetting part) was an exercise I had done with a Catholic supper club. In spite of my memory loss, the prayer was answered.

"Joe, they're looking for a Catholic therapist to host a radio show," a friend told me. "Hmm," I thought, "I've never done radio. Perfect." I sent in a fun demo and then spent the next couple of weeks trying to convince the producers that they would be making a huge mistake by hiring me. Luckily they didn't listen to my fear and instead focused on my potential.

Not even a year into the show, we had experienced incredible growth. They loosened up the reins and gave me tremendous liberty. They had a "dump button" if someone called in and said something ridiculous, but I think I was the only one at real risk of being "dumped".

Even though I worked very hard to prepare myself for each topic I would discuss, I sweated bullets over whether I would make any sense. Right before the start of each show, I would kneel and pray, "Lord, I have no idea what's going to come out of my mouth. Help!" Honestly, I was sure that I was unqualified for the task at hand, yet I trusted that God would work through His imperfect vessel and get the job done anyway. Each show was an exercise in faith and hope, which aren't the absence of doubt and fear but allow us, despite our doubt and fear, to act with the confidence that all will be well.

And all was well. People called in and shared their stories about everything from rape, addiction, broken lives, and families, to blessings, hope, grace, and belief. And I got to share in it all. It was incredibly humbling. But most humbling was sharing Christ's story—the one about forgiveness, redemption, and unconditional love. And I found that the good news is as relevant, powerful, and healing as ever.

After the show was under way, the host of the supper club gave me the prayer in the sealed envelope that I had forgotten about. It read: "I pray, Lord, that You open the door for me to participate in Your ministry, allowing me to use my creative gifts in a more significant way."

Thanks be to God that He had not forgotten me, even though I often forget Him. Daily I had prayed for my family, my boys, but I learned through this answered prayer that it was all right to send one up for myself occasionally.

In addition to the radio show, I continued to see clients in my counseling practice. Friends asked if it was difficult to listen to other people's problems given our own circumstances. If therapy involved only listening to problem-saturated stories, then perhaps being a counselor would have been tough for me. But therapy also involves the privilege of entering into people's lives, meeting them where they are, and walking with them as they move toward solutions and healing. Being a therapist is, for the most part, invigorating.

I was happily at work in my therapy office at Saint Jude's (the parish whose grammar school John sadly had to leave), when there came an insistent knock on the door. Apologizing profusely to my clients, I answered the door, prepared to give directions to the bathroom. I wish. Instead, Monica, a dear friend of my family, stood before me with worry written all over her face.

"Lori needs you at the hospital. They need to put a tracheal tube in John."

Suppressing as much emotion as possible, I raced to the hospital. By the time I arrived, John was already on a respirator.

"I'm so sorry. I'm so sorry," Lori said when she greeted me.

A few days earlier, when Lori was putting John to bed, tears started running down his cheeks.

"Is something hurting, John?" Lori asked him.

He didn't seem to be in pain. And he didn't have a fever. But something was definitely wrong.

That morning, Lori noticed that John's temperature was rising. Just to play it safe, she took him to the hospital after I left for the office—the intuition of a loving mother. When they arrived at the emergency room, the tears began rolling down John's face again. Then he vomited and started choking.

"Tell me what to do, Mom," the doctor said.

As John gasped for air, Lori knew she couldn't let his beautiful, grace-filled life end this way. And I wasn't there. Losing him without the other parent present was one of our greatest fears.

Lori left the room for a moment while John was intubated. Then the respirator began to do the breathing that he could not quite manage on his own. It provided momentary comfort.

"I think there's a little pneumonia," the doctor said. "We can beat this."

"Let's hope so," we thought, because the decision to turn off the respirator could possibly be even harder than the decision to turn it on.

Lori and I had discussed respirators before. We would let God take our boys whenever He was ready to do so, we had decided. We were not going to hold on to them with extraordinary methods of care, with everything science and technology has to offer, when nature said enough. A given treatment would be accepted if it added to the quality of their lives and not simply to the quantity of their days. But these conversations were theoretical. The demands of real-time decision-making, however, were far more brutal.

A couple of days later, they were able to remove the breathing tube, but not the complications and the discomfort. John's lungs kept filling with fluid, and he had lost his natural ability to cough it up. Frequently his lungs needed to be cleared by suction tubes run up his nose and into his lungs. It was unbearable to watch, and far worse to bear after the umpteenth time. But we were not going anywhere, at least not yet.

Days stretched on. We slept, ate, cried, and prayed by John's side. The doctors were kind, but their words were painfully honest. The end was near.

And then his bowels seemed to stop.

I will never forget John's last laugh when I joked about his noisy high-tech bed.

"You sound like Uncle Mike's Harley, John. Let's call him up and challenge him to a race." And the smile spread across his face.

But then the breathing tube went back in, and John was back on the respirator.

A day later we phoned Mark Dodson, a brilliant doctor whom we had known for a long time. The Dodsons had lived next door to me in Florida. Lori and I each choked out a sentence or two between tears.

"Joe," he said, "we can't do everything. But we can make patients really comfortable. He won't know he's supposed to be struggling for breath."

Lori understood, but even she needed to hear from someone who loved us that the time had come to end extraordinary medical treatment and to provide only palliative care. How we spoke the words to the doctors, I don't know, but we told them it was time let God have John.

Many friends came in to say their good-byes. Father Jim, from Saint Jude's, came frequently. At a moment when he and I and John were the only ones in the room, I asked if he would hear my confession. At last I was able to confess something I had held inside for a long time, perhaps because it was a somewhat inarticulate and nagging feeling like a pebble in the shoe—too small to see, but big enough to cause pain. It was the conclusion I had drawn from believing the suggestion of Job's friends: bad things don't happen to good people.

"I did this," I said to Father Jim through burning tears. "God has cursed me, my sons, because of my sins, my life."

"Oh, Joe," Father said tenderly. "Look at his beauty. This magnificent boy. I see no curse. Only blessing here."

As he passed by, he saw a man blind from his birth. And his disciples asked him, "Rabbi, who sinned, this man or his parents, that he was born blind?" Jesus answered, "It was not that this man sinned, or his parents, but that the works of God might be made manifest in him. We must work the works of him who sent me, while it is day; night comes, when no one can work. As long as I am in the world, I am the light of the world." (Jn 9:1–5)

God's magnificent plan for us cannot be reduced to our simplistic explanations. In times of weakness and loss, I sometimes blamed myself. But God had accomplished in John's life what I couldn't even have imagined. I could choose to live in the darkness of self-imposed guilt, or I could live in the light of a loving God. Each day, we are all given that choice.

At last the moment had arrived. With our hearts breaking, we watched as the nurses stopped John's pacemaker. "You should leave the room as we remove the breathing tube," they said.

Lori responded first: "We aren't leaving." And we didn't. We hadn't walked away from the tough stuff for years. This was no time to start. We weren't the only ones crying. Someone dressed in hospital garb grabbed our hands and prayed with us.

I had never loved so much. Lori. John. Ben. I had never felt so close to my wife. I had never witnessed anyone as brave as she was in that moment. I doubt I ever will.

After they had removed all the medical equipment, strangely, we felt we had John back. We expected him to die immediately, but he did not. Friends continuously brought us food so that we wouldn't have to leave his side. We slept (sort of) by his side in hospital chairs. We competed with each other to be on the side on which he laid his head so that we could relish an unobstructed view of his angelic face. We rarely let go of his hand. He was unconscious and comfortable. And I was consoled by his warm hand wrapped in mine.

Brother Tom from Chaminade visited. So did Andy and John's other dear friends. "Don't abandon me," Ben pleaded with them. They wouldn't.

Never one to shy away from strong emotions, Ben wailed, rolled around on the floor, and cried. Yet somehow he managed some gentle good-byes. "You'll be okay, John," he said. "You'll be with your grandpas and Cameron. You'll be able to see and run."

When Pope Francis was visiting America, we decided to turn on the television. We joined the rest of the world as it watched him, fascinated and enthralled.

I noticed on the board affixed to the wall John's care plan along with the names of his nurses. One of them was a classmate of his from Saint Jude's. She was a brand-new nurse, and John was one of her first patients. Full circle.

Also on the board was "*Star Wars* and *Lion King*". Both of these stories were so important to our boys, especially John. A few years before John had asked me if he could meet Luke Skywalker.

"Um ... I'm not sure about that, John."

Behind my answer, I realized, was the kind of trepidation that would have gotten Luke into trouble with Yoda. So I reached out to a friend of mine, Ed Solomon. Ed didn't own a space ship or any other kind of ship as far as I knew, but he was a successful writer in Hollywood with imagination and connections, and he generously agreed to call the agent of Mark Hamill, the actor who had become an international star by playing Skywalker.

Hamill's agent set the stage for disappointment by telling Ed, "I'll ask, but ..." Two minutes later, however, he called back to say that "Luke" had agreed to meet John.

In a quiet park in Malibu John asked "Luke" question after question, repeating himself numerous times, and Hamill patiently answered each one with tenderness and affection. His kindness, which was so literally out of the blue, was yet another proof that we were not alone.

Ben and John watched *Star Wars* together one last time in the hospital. Of course, it wouldn't do for them to watch episode 3. John couldn't bear to see Anakin turn to the dark side. We would allow no darkness in his sacred space of light. After the movie, Ben laid his head on John's chest and said, "Good-bye, John. Don't worry. You're going to have a lot of fun in heaven."

Someone came to take Ben home, and as he left, he seemed, well, peaceful.

Later that evening, Lori said, "Don't go anywhere, John. I have to get a Diet Coke." Typical John, he obeyed. Then his breathing changed as Lori came back into the room. "Turn the TV off, Joe. I think he's dying," she said. The pope was waving good-bye to the crowd as I clicked off the television. Seconds later, John breathed his last.

# 40

# Focused on the Prize

How do you prepare for the unimaginable? Intellectually, pretty early in life, we recognize that all living things must give way to death. We see that movies have a beginning, a middle, and an end, as do all stories. School years come and go. As we grow older we suffer bigger losses—jobs and relationships and loved ones who precede us.

But to watch the final breath taken by one's own child—some say the death of a child is the toughest loss of all.

I remember the first breath John took. Was I prepared for it? No. Not really. Although I understood that Lori was pregnant and I was a father, I didn't really get it. Holding John's tiny body against mine; smelling his sweet baby's breath rise up and enter my body through my nostrils; feeling his racing, beating heart against my chest—I experienced it all, yet it was all surreal.

And so was his death.

We left the hospital, quietly, but if tears could make noise, their sound would be as loud as a bomb exploding. Getting into our car, we looked at the hospital, at where his room was. The light was on, but he was gone.

Back at home, we awoke Ben. Hand in hand we took our familiar walk through the neighborhood greenbelt, but everything about our conversation was unfamiliar.

"He is with your dad, Dad, and Papa," Ben said. Then more tears. The mind can fathom ending, although inadequately. But the heart is made to reject endings; it cries out for eternity. With our hearts, we feel that death is not an end, but a transformation into new and better life. This is hope, and for a Christian it is the hope that is based on our faith in Christ's Resurrection.

Another gathering, in Saint Maximilian Kolbe Catholic Church: friends and family were present, except my mom, who was too sick to make the trip, and my brother John, who stayed with her.

We met John's coffin at the front of the church, and Ben, alongside his uncles, led it to the altar. Also there were Fathers Dave and Ken, who had met us at the front of Saint Monica's twenty-four years earlier for Mass.

A friend, Derrick, sang Leonard Cohen's "Hallelujah", a version of the song that represents what we believe as Christians.

Lori and I both shared stories, some of the same stories I've shared in this book. We laughed and cried. Again, I could know no braver person than my wife as she continued to take one step at a time. My final words, as I pointed to the huge cross on which the body of our Lord hung lifeless, were these: "Without what He did, it is all meaningless."

After the funeral I was speaking to a dear friend, Michael. He is Protestant and, as such, was completely unfamiliar with the Rosary. During the vigil the night before the funeral, he said, he had "lost himself, not really sure what it was supposed to mean." But he "submitted to the emotion of the moment and the ritual" and experienced a "powerful, powerful, clear, amazing image of the most vibrant John." He said John was "so robust and healthy and full of life and had his signature, effervescent smile." Yet this smile was "one hundred times more powerful than his real smile. It was just such a strong image of a beautiful, content, young man."

Two months later, we celebrated Ben's twenty-first birthday. Many came and offered an unbelievable outpouring of love. The following morning, Ben came and said, "He came to me. John came to me last night."

"What did he look like? What did he say?"

Ben said John was white and gold and told him, "I'm okay, Ben. I'm okay."

John's words didn't take away Ben's pain, but Ben could hold the pain because he was given a glimpse of the future, or rather a glimpse of heaven. Like God, heaven is beyond time and space. In some mysterious way, the souls who are with God are actually all around us at every moment in what Catholics call the communion of saints.

Several weeks later, during Mass at Saint Maximilian, Ben leaned over and whispered to me that he saw John again. But Ben is blind. Or is he? He pointed up to the cross and said, "He was right over there." Pointing to the side of the church, he added, "Then he flew out there." Did Ben "see" what he wanted to see? Did God offer him a vision of what He wanted him to see? I don't know. God alone knows.

How do you prepare for the inevitable death of those you love? How do you prepare for your inevitable death? My answer: you live. Completely. Daringly. Adventurously. You love, knowing that love is the only thing that matters. It's a choice to love in this way. But so long as love remains, life continues.

When you enter almost any Catholic church you are faced with the powerful image of Christ on the Cross. Death. But for those who believe, it is the one death that signals life, that turns all death into a gateway to eternal life.

Ben didn't stop, and neither did we. We did not get over the pain of John's death. We learned to hold it and to carry on. Ben said he wanted to go to college. Why not? All his friends were going. Ben remained the constant reminder that the heart can propel a person forward when his mind and body say, "Impossible."

A young friend, Abby (the sister of John's buddy Andy), was attending California Lutheran University, only about fifteen minutes away from our home. She knew of Ben's dream and went directly to the administration. As a result, we had an admittance interview with the associate dean, Scott Silverman. It was reminiscent of our interview at Chaminade. With numerous newspapers (and National Public Radio) recording the orientation day, Ben was in.

Ben's fuel for adventure has yet to run low, but his body and brain have slowed. One evening, sitting on the back patio, listening to music, I saw Ben standing in the kitchen. I called to him to come join me.

"I can't," he said. "My legs won't move."

I walked in, gave him my arm, a touch, and his feet slowly began to move forward. How much more time will we be given with him? I don't know. How will tomorrow work? I don't know that either, but I do know that it will work.

We set up a small scholarship at Chaminade, the John Sikorra Courageous Heart Award. It is not based on academic achievement or athletic prowess but is given to a student who lives his faith and life courageously.

A month before John died, Lori had decided to go back to school to get her nurse practitioner license. She was admitted into the prestigious program at UCLA. But given our family situation, she had to let it go. The following year, she reapplied. Some faculty thought she was too old, had too much going on in her life. Without the lessons the boys had taught us, she might have agreed. But what we can really accomplish is not based on self-confidence. Personally, I think self-confidence is overrated. God-confidence, however, takes us beyond what we think we can accomplish.

Lori's favorite place has remained Serra Retreat Center in beautiful Malibu. She has a special place there to sit, to connect, because friends got together and donated a bench with John's name on it for one of the beautiful gardens. It is near a statue of Mary. Once in a while, Lori is greeted by a noisy bunch of wild parrots. With a smile, and with tears, she remembers how John would try to shush them.

We are all just passing through. There's no reason to get too comfortable here. If we did, we would never be willing to let go. A glorious existence awaits us. No one needs to tell me it will be all right. I know. If we learn to address our fears with faith, love, and laughter, we can learn to defy gravity.

Days before John passed, while watching his chest move up and down with slow rhythmic breaths, I wrote what I thought he would like, and what my feeble imagination could muster, to announce his passing. Lori posted it on Facebook the morning following his death:

> On September 24, at 9 P.M., a thunderous crack was heard that rocked the heavens. The sound was that of a Louisville slugger ripping the leather off a baseball. John dropped the bat, flashed his dimpled smile, and with bright green eyes watched as the ball screamed into the distance. As it sailed, it was set ablaze with brilliant and unimaginable colors. A choir of angels erupted with cheers as the mighty Sikorra began his trot around the bases. The brightness of a thousand suns lit his way. As he stepped onto the final plate, Jesus spoke the words, "The greatest hit ever. Welcome home."

Our journey is not yet done. The days, however, are passing quickly. Only a few remain. I do not count them, for my eyes are focused on what lies ahead. I see a shining light upon a hill. With vision that only faith can provide, I see my boys walking toward it. Then running. I too hope to reach the light after I have finished running the race. I hope to hear the words, "Good job, Joe. Come, enter into life. Real life." And from my son John, wrapped once again in my arms, in an everlasting embrace, I hope to hear, "I've been waiting for you, Dad. Come, we'll show you around. You're about to see things that you could never have imagined."

# ACKNOWLEDGMENTS

So many individuals, doctors, families, and organizations have helped me and my family that it would have been impossible to name them all in this story. They know who they are, and I would like to take this opportunity to thank them again.

There are some organizations that deserve special mention: Beyond Batten Disease Foundation and Batten Disease Support and Research Association. Since they are on the forefront of battling Batten disease and assisting those suffering from it, the proceeds of this book will be donated to them.